ARCADIA

ARCADIA
Tom Stoppard

ff

faber and faber

LONDON NEW YORK

Faber and Faber, Inc.
An affiliate of Farrar, Straus and Giroux
19 Union Square West, New York 10003

First published in 1993
by Faber and Faber Limited
3 Queen Square, London WC1N 3AU
Reprinted with corrections, 1993

Tom Stoppard is hereby identified as author of this work in accordance with
Section 77 of the Copyright, Designs and Patents Act of 1988.

A CIP record for this book is available from the British Library
and from the Library of Congress

Hardcover ISBN-10: 0-571-16933-3
Paperback ISBN-13: 978-0-571-16934-4
Paperback ISBN-10: 0-571-16934-1

www.fsgbooks.com

17   19   21   23   25   24   22   20   18   16

CHARACTERS

(in order of appearance)

THOMASINA COVERLY, aged thirteen, later sixteen
SEPTIMUS HODGE, her tutor, aged twenty-two, later twenty-five
JELLABY, a butler, middle-aged
EZRA CHATER, a poet, aged thirty-one
RICHARD NOAKES, a landscape architect, middle-aged
LADY CROOM, middle thirties
CAPT. BRICE, RN, middle thirties
HANNAH JARVIS, an author, late thirties
CHLOË COVERLY, aged eighteen
BERNARD NIGHTINGALE, a don, late thirties
VALENTINE COVERLY, aged twenty-five to thirty
GUS COVERLY, aged fifteen
AUGUSTUS COVERLY, aged fifteen

Arcadia opened at the Lyttelton Theatre, Royal National Theatre, on 13 April 1993. The cast was as follows:

THOMASINA COVERLY	Emma Fielding
SEPTIMUS HODGE	Rufus Sewell
JELLABY	Allan Mitchell
EZRA CHATER	Derek Hutchinson
RICHARD NOAKES	Sidney Livingstone
LADY CROOM	Harriet Walter
CAPTAIN BRICE, RN	Graham Sinclair
HANNAH JARVIS	Felicity Kendal
CHLOË COVERLY	Harriet Harrison
BERNARD NIGHTINGALE	Bill Nighy
VALENTINE COVERLY	Samuel West
GUS COVERLY ⎫	Timothy Matthews
AUGUSTUS COVERLY ⎭	

Director	Trevor Nunn
Designer	Mark Thompson
Lighting	Paul Pyant
Music	Jeremy Sams

ACT ONE

SCENE ONE

A room on the garden front of a very large country house in Derbyshire in April 1809. Nowadays, the house would be called a stately home. The upstage wall is mainly tall, shapely, uncurtained windows, one or more of which work as doors. Nothing much need be said or seen of the exterior beyond. We come to learn that the house stands in the typical English park of the time. Perhaps we see an indication of this, perhaps only light and air and sky.

The room looks bare despite the large table which occupies the centre of it. The table, the straight-backed chairs and, the only other item of furniture, the architect's stand or reading stand, would all be collectable pieces now but here, on an uncarpeted wood floor, they have no more pretension than a schoolroom, which is indeed the main use of this room at this time. What elegance there is, is architectural, and nothing is impressive but the scale. There is a door in each of the side walls. These are closed, but one of the french windows is open to a bright but sunless morning.

There are two people, each busy with books and paper and pen and ink, separately occupied. The pupil is THOMASINA COVERLY, *aged 13. The tutor is* SEPTIMUS HODGE, *aged 22. Each has an open book. Hers is a slim mathematics primer. His is a handsome thick quarto, brand new, a vanity production, with little tapes to tie when the book is closed. His loose papers, etc, are kept in a stiff-backed portfolio which also ties up with tapes.*

Septimus has a tortoise which is sleepy enough to serve as a paperweight.

Elsewhere on the table there is an old-fashioned theodolite and also some other books stacked up.

THOMASINA: Septimus, what is carnal embrace?

SEPTIMUS: Carnal embrace is the practice of throwing one's arms around a side of beef.

THOMASINA: Is that all?

SEPTIMUS: No . . . a shoulder of mutton, a haunch of venison well hugged, an embrace of grouse . . . *caro, carnis*; feminine; flesh.

THOMASINA: Is it a sin?

SEPTIMUS: Not necessarily, my lady, but when carnal embrace is sinful it is a sin of the flesh, QED. We had *caro* in our Gallic Wars – 'The Britons live on milk and meat' – '*lacte et carne vivunt*'. I am sorry that the seed fell on stony ground.

THOMASINA: That was the sin of Onan, wasn't it, Septimus?

SEPTIMUS: Yes. He was giving his brother's wife a Latin lesson and she was hardly the wiser after it than before. I thought you were finding a proof for Fermat's last theorem.

THOMASINA: It is very difficult, Septimus. You will have to show me how.

SEPTIMUS: If I knew how, there would be no need to ask *you*. Fermat's last theorem has kept people busy for a hundred and fifty years, and I hoped it would keep *you* busy long enough for me to read Mr Chater's poem in praise of love with only the distraction of its own absurdities.

THOMASINA: Our Mr Chater has written a poem?

SEPTIMUS: He believes he has written a poem, yes. I can see that there might be more carnality in your algebra than in Mr Chater's 'Couch of Eros'.

THOMASINA: Oh, it was not my algebra. I heard Jellaby telling cook that Mrs Chater was discovered in carnal embrace in the gazebo.

SEPTIMUS: (*Pause*) Really? With whom, did Jellaby happen to say? (THOMASINA *considers this with a puzzled frown.*)

THOMASINA: What do you mean, with whom?

SEPTIMUS: With what? Exactly so. The idea is absurd. Where did this story come from?

THOMASINA: Mr Noakes.

SEPTIMUS: Mr Noakes!

THOMASINA: Papa's landskip gardener. He was taking bearings in the garden when he saw – through his spyglass – Mrs Chater in the gazebo in carnal embrace.

SEPTIMUS: And do you mean to tell me that Mr Noakes told the butler?

THOMASINA: No. Mr Noakes told Mr Chater. *Jellaby* was told by the groom, who overheard Mr Noakes telling Mr Chater, in the stable yard.

2

SEPTIMUS: Mr Chater being engaged in closing the stable door.

THOMASINA: What do you mean, Septimus?

SEPTIMUS: So, thus far, the only people who know about this are Mr Noakes the landskip architect, the groom, the butler, the cook and, of course, Mrs Chater's husband, the poet.

THOMASINA: And Arthur who was cleaning the silver, and the bootboy. And now you.

SEPTIMUS: Of course. What else did he say?

THOMASINA: Mr Noakes?

SEPTIMUS: No, not Mr Noakes. Jellaby. You heard Jellaby telling the cook.

THOMASINA: Cook hushed him almost as soon as he started. Jellaby did not see that I was being allowed to finish yesterday's upstairs' rabbit pie before I came to my lesson. I think you have not been candid with me, Septimus. A gazebo is not, after all, a meat larder.

SEPTIMUS: I never said my definition was complete.

THOMASINA: Is carnal embrace kissing?

SEPTIMUS: Yes.

THOMASINA: And throwing one's arms around Mrs Chater?

SEPTIMUS: Yes. Now, Fermat's last theorem –

THOMASINA: I thought as much. I hope you are ashamed.

SEPTIMUS: I, my lady?

THOMASINA: If *you* do not teach me the true meaning of things, who will?

SEPTIMUS: Ah. Yes, I am ashamed. Carnal embrace is sexual congress, which is the insertion of the male genital organ into the female genital organ for purposes of procreation and pleasure. Fermat's last theorem, by contrast, asserts that when x, y and z are whole numbers each raised to power of n, the sum of the first two can never equal the third when n is greater than 2.

(*Pause.*)

THOMASINA: Eurghhh!

SEPTIMUS: Nevertheless, that is the theorem.

THOMASINA: It is disgusting and incomprehensible. Now when I am grown to practise it myself I shall never do so without thinking of you.

SEPTIMUS: Thank you very much, my lady. Was Mrs Chater down this morning?

THOMASINA: No. Tell me more about sexual congress.

SEPTIMUS: There is nothing more to be said about sexual congress.

THOMASINA: Is it the same as love?

SEPTIMUS: Oh no, it is much nicer than that.

(*One of the side doors leads to the music room. It is the other side door which now opens to admit* JELLABY, *the butler*.)

I am teaching, Jellaby.

JELLABY: Beg your pardon, Mr Hodge, Mr Chater said it was urgent you receive his letter.

SEPTIMUS: Oh, very well. (SEPTIMUS *takes the letter*.) Thank you. (*And to dismiss* JELLABY.) Thank you.

JELLABY: (*Holding his ground*) Mr Chater asked me to bring him your answer.

SEPTIMUS: My answer?

(*He opens the letter. There is no envelope as such, but there is a 'cover' which, folded and sealed, does the same service.*
SEPTIMUS *tosses the cover negligently aside and reads*.)
Well, my answer is that as is my custom and my duty to his lordship I am engaged until a quarter to twelve in the education of his daughter. When I am done, and if Mr Chater is still there, I will be happy to wait upon him in – (*he checks the letter*) – in the gunroom.

JELLABY: I will tell him so, thank you, sir.

(SEPTIMUS *folds the letter and places it between the pages of 'The Couch of Eros'*.)

THOMASINA: What is for dinner, Jellaby?

JELLABY: Boiled ham and cabbages, my lady, and a rice pudding.

THOMASINA: Oh, goody.

(JELLABY *leaves*.)

SEPTIMUS: Well, so much for Mr Noakes. He puts himself forward as a gentleman, a philosopher of the picturesque, a visionary who can move mountains and cause lakes, but in the scheme of the garden he is as the serpent.

THOMASINA: When you stir your rice pudding, Septimus, the spoonful of jam spreads itself round making red trails like

4

the picture of a meteor in my astronomical atlas. But if you stir backward, the jam will not come together again. Indeed, the pudding does not notice and continues to turn pink just as before. Do you think this is odd?

SEPTIMUS: No.

THOMASINA: Well, I do. You cannot stir things apart.

SEPTIMUS: No more you can, time must needs run backward, and since it will not, we must stir our way onward mixing as we go, disorder out of disorder into disorder until pink is complete, unchanging and unchangeable, and we are done with it for ever. This is known as free will or self-determination.

(*He picks up the tortoise and moves it a few inches as though it had strayed, on top of some loose papers, and admonishes it.*)

Sit!

THOMASINA: Septimus, do you think God is a Newtonian?

SEPTIMUS: An Etonian? Almost certainly, I'm afraid. We must ask your brother to make it his first enquiry.

THOMASINA: No, Septimus, a Newtonian. Septimus! Am I the first person to have thought of this?

SEPTIMUS: No.

THOMASINA: I have not said yet.

SEPTIMUS: 'If everything from the furthest planet to the smallest atom of our brain acts according to Newton's law of motion, what becomes of free will?'

THOMASINA: No.

SEPTIMUS: God's will.

THOMASINA: No.

SEPTIMUS: Sin.

THOMASINA: (*Derisively*) No!

SEPTIMUS: Very well.

THOMASINA: If you could stop every atom in its position and direction, and if your mind could comprehend all the actions thus suspended, then if you were really, *really* good at algebra you could write the formula for all the future; and although nobody can be so clever as to do it, the formula must exist just as if one could.

SEPTIMUS: (*Pause*) Yes. (*Pause.*) Yes, as far as I know, you are the first person to have thought of this. (*Pause. With an effort.*) In the margin of his copy of *Arithmetica*, Fermat wrote that he had discovered a wonderful proof of his theorem but, the margin being too narrow for his purpose, did not have room to write it down. The note was found after his death, and from that day to this –

THOMASINA: Oh! I see now! The answer is perfectly obvious.

SEPTIMUS: This time you may have overreached yourself.

(*The door is opened, somewhat violently.* CHATER *enters.*)
Mr Chater! Perhaps my message miscarried. I will be at liberty at a quarter to twelve, if that is convenient.

CHATER: It is not convenient, sir. My business will not wait.

SEPTIMUS: Then I suppose you have Lord Croom's opinion that your business is more important than his daughter's lesson.

CHATER: I do not, but, if you like, I will ask his lordship to settle the point.

SEPTIMUS: (*Pause*) My lady, take Fermat into the music room. There will be an extra spoonful of jam if you find his proof.

THOMASINA: There is no proof, Septimus. The thing that is perfectly obvious is that the note in the margin was a joke to make you all mad.

(THOMASINA *leaves.*)

SEPTIMUS: Now, sir, what is this business that cannot wait?

CHATER: I think you know it, sir. You have insulted my wife.

SEPTIMUS: Insulted her? That would deny my nature, my conduct, and the admiration in which I hold Mrs Chater.

CHATER: I have heard of your admiration, sir! You insulted my wife in the gazebo yesterday evening!

SEPTIMUS: You are mistaken. I made love to your wife in the gazebo. She asked me to meet her there, I have her note somewhere, I dare say I could find it for you, and if someone is putting it about that I did not turn up, by God, sir, it is a slander.

CHATER: You damned lecher! You would drag down a lady's reputation to make a refuge for your cowardice. It will not do! I am calling you out!

SEPTIMUS: Chater! Chater, Chater, Chater! My dear friend!

CHATER: You dare to call me that. I demand satisfaction!

6

SEPTIMUS: Mrs Chater demanded satisfaction and now you are
demanding satisfaction. I cannot spend my time day and
night satisfying the demands of the Chater family. As for
your wife's reputation, it stands where it ever stood.

CHATER: You blackguard!

SEPTIMUS: I assure you. Mrs Chater is charming and spirited,
with a pleasing voice and a dainty step, she is the epitome of
all the qualities society applauds in her sex – and yet her chief
renown is for a readiness that keeps her in a state of tropical
humidity as would grow orchids in her drawers in January.

CHATER: Damn you, Hodge, I will not listen to this! Will you
fight or not?

SEPTIMUS: (*Definitively*) Not! There are no more than two or
three poets of the first rank now living, and I will not shoot
one of them dead over a perpendicular poke in a gazebo with
a woman whose reputation could not be adequately defended
with a platoon of musketry deployed by rota.

CHATER: Ha! You say so! Who are the others? In your opinion? –
no – no – ! – this goes very ill, Hodge. I will not be flattered
out of my course. You say so, do you?

SEPTIMUS: I do. And I would say the same to Milton were he not
already dead. Not the part about his wife, of course –

CHATER: But among the living? Mr Southey?

SEPTIMUS: Southey I would have shot on sight.

CHATER: (*Shaking his head sadly*) Yes, he has fallen off. I admired
'Thalaba' *quite*, but 'Madoc', (*he chuckles*) oh dear me! – but
we are straying from the business here – you took advantage
of Mrs Chater, and if that were not bad enough, it appears
every stableboy and scullery maid on the strength –

SEPTIMUS: Damn me! Have you not listened to a word I said?

CHATER: I have heard you, sir, and I will not deny I welcome
your regard, God knows one is little appreciated if one stands
outside the coterie of hacks and placemen who surround
Jeffrey and the *Edinburgh* –

SEPTIMUS: My dear Chater, they judge a poet by the seating plan
of Lord Holland's table!

CHATER: By heaven, you are right! And I would very much like
to know the name of the scoundrel who slandered my verse

7

drama 'The Maid of Turkey' in the *Piccadilly Recreation*, too!

SEPTIMUS: 'The Maid of Turkey'! I have it by my bedside! When I cannot sleep I take up 'The Maid of Turkey' like an old friend!

CHATER: (*Gratified*) There you are! And the scoundrel wrote he would not give it to his dog for dinner were it covered in bread sauce and stuffed with chestnuts. When Mrs Chater read that, she wept, sir, and would not give herself to me for a fortnight – which recalls me to my purpose –

SEPTIMUS: The new poem, however, will make your name perpetual –

CHATER: Whether it do or not –

SEPTIMUS: It is not a question, sir. No coterie can oppose the acclamation of the reading public. 'The Couch of Eros' will take the town.

CHATER: Is that your estimation?

SEPTIMUS: It is my intent.

CHATER: Is it, is it? Well, well! I do not understand you.

SEPTIMUS: You see I have an early copy – sent to me for review. I say review, but I speak of an extensive appreciation of your gifts and your rightful place in English literature.

CHATER: Well, I must say. That is certainly . . . You have written it?

SEPTIMUS: (*Crisply*) Not yet.

CHATER: Ah. And how long does . . . ?

SEPTIMUS: To be done right, it first requires a careful re-reading of your book, of both your books, several readings, together with outlying works for an exhibition of deference or disdain as the case merits. I make notes, of course, I order my thoughts, and finally, when all is ready and I am *calm in my mind* . . .

CHATER: (*Shrewdly*) Did Mrs Chater know of this before she – before you –

SEPTIMUS: I think she very likely did.

CHATER: (*Triumphantly*) There is nothing that woman would not do for me! Now you have an insight to her character. Yes, by God, she is a wife to me, sir!

SEPTIMUS: For that alone, I would not make her a widow.

CHATER: Captain Brice once made the same observation!

SEPTIMUS: Captain Brice did?

CHATER: Mr Hodge, allow me to inscribe your copy in happy anticipation. Lady Thomasina's pen will serve us.

SEPTIMUS: Your connection with Lord and Lady Croom you owe to your fighting her ladyship's brother?

CHATER: No! It was all nonsense, sir – a canard! But a fortunate mistake, sir. It brought me the patronage of a captain of His Majesty's Navy and the brother of a countess. I do not think Mr Walter Scott can say as much, and here I am, a respected guest at Sidley Park.

SEPTIMUS: Well, sir, you can say you have received satisfaction. (CHATER *is already inscribing the book, using the pen and ink-pot on the table.* NOAKES *enters through the door used by* CHATER. *He carries rolled-up plans.* CHATER, *inscribing, ignores* NOAKES. NOAKES *on seeing the occupants, panics.*)

NOAKES: Oh!

SEPTIMUS: Ah, Mr Noakes! – my muddy-mettled rascal! Where's your spyglass?

NOAKES: I beg your leave – I thought her ladyship – excuse me – (*He is beating an embarrassed retreat when he becomes rooted by* CHATER's *voice.* CHATER *reads his inscription in ringing tones.*)

CHATER: 'To my friend Septimus Hodge, who stood up and gave his best on behalf of the Author – Ezra Chater, at Sidley Park, Derbyshire, April 10th, 1809.' (*Giving the book to* SEPTIMUS.) There, sir – something to show your grandchildren!

SEPTIMUS: This is more than I deserve, this is handsome, what do you say, Noakes? (*They are interrupted by the appearance, outside the windows, of* LADY CROOM *and* CAPTAIN EDWARD BRICE, RN. *Her first words arrive through the open door.*)

LADY CROOM: Oh, no! Not the gazebo! (*She enters, followed by* BRICE *who carries a leatherbound sketch book.*) Mr Noakes! What is this I hear?

BRICE: Not only the gazebo, but the boat-house, the Chinese bridge, the shrubbery –

9

CHATER: By God, sir! Not possible!

BRICE: Mr Noakes will have it so.

SEPTIMUS: Mr Noakes, this is monstrous!

LADY CROOM: I am glad to hear it from *you*, Mr Hodge.

THOMASINA: (*Opening the door from the music room*) May I return now?

SEPTIMUS: (*Attempting to close the door*) Not just yet –

LADY CROOM: Yes, let her stay. A lesson in folly is worth two in wisdom.

(BRICE *takes the sketch book to the reading stand, where he lays it open. The sketch book is the work of* MR NOAKES, *who is obviously an admirer of Humphry Repton's 'Red Books'. The pages, drawn in watercolours, show 'before' and 'after' views of the landscape, and the pages are cunningly cut to allow the latter to be superimposed over portions of the former, though Repton did it the other way round.*)

BRICE: Is Sidley Park to be an Englishman's garden or the haunt of Corsican brigands?

SEPTIMUS: Let us not hyperbolize, sir.

BRICE: It is rape, sir!

NOAKES: (*Defending himself.*) It is the modern style.

CHATER: (*Under the same misapprehension as* SEPTIMUS) Regrettable, of course, but so it is.

(THOMASINA *has gone to examine the sketch book.*)

LADY CROOM: Mr Chater, you show too much submission. Mr Hodge, I appeal to you.

SEPTIMUS: Madam, I regret the gazebo, I sincerely regret the gazebo – and the boat-house up to a point – but the Chinese bridge, fantasy! – and the shrubbery I reject with contempt! Mr Chater! – would you take the word of a jumped-up jobbing gardener who sees carnal embrace in every nook and cranny of the landskip!

THOMASINA: Septimus, they are not speaking of carnal embrace, are you, Mama?

LADY CROOM: Certainly not. What do you know of carnal embrace?

THOMASINA: Everything, thanks to Septimus. In my opinion, Mr Noakes's scheme for the garden is perfect. It is a Salvator!

LADY CROOM: What does she mean?

NOAKES: (*Answering the wrong question*) Salvator Rosa, your
     ladyship, the painter. He is indeed the very exemplar of the
     picturesque style.
BRICE: Hodge, what is this?
SEPTIMUS: She speaks from innocence not from experience.
BRICE: You call it innocence? Has he ruined you, child?
     (*Pause.*)
SEPTIMUS: Answer your uncle!
THOMASINA: (*To* SEPTIMUS.) How is a ruined child different
     from a ruined castle?
SEPTIMUS: On such questions I defer to Mr Noakes.
NOAKES: (*Out of his depth*) A ruined castle is picturesque,
     certainly.
SEPTIMUS: That is the main difference. (*To* BRICE) I teach the
     classical authors. If I do not elucidate their meaning, who
     will?
BRICE: As her tutor you have a duty to keep her in ignorance.
LADY CROOM: Do not dabble in paradox, Edward, it puts you in
     danger of fortuitous wit. Thomasina, wait in your bedroom.
THOMASINA: (*Retiring*) Yes, mama. I did not intend to get you
     into trouble, Septimus. I am very sorry for it. It is plain that
     there are some things a girl is allowed to understand, and
     these include the whole of algebra, but there are others, such
     as embracing a side of beef, that must be kept from her until
     she is old enough to have a carcass of her own.
LADY CROOM: One moment.
BRICE: What is she talking about?
LADY CROOM: Meat.
BRICE: Meat?
LADY CROOM: Thomasina, you had better remain. Your
     knowledge of the picturesque obviously exceeds anything the
     rest of us can offer. Mr Hodge, ignorance should be like an
     empty vessel waiting to be filled at the well of truth – not a
     cabinet of vulgar curios. Mr Noakes – now at last it is your
     turn –
NOAKES: Thank you, your ladyship –
LADY CROOM: Your drawing is a very wonderful transformation.
     I would not have recognized my own garden but for your

ingenious book – is it not? – look! Here is the Park as it appears to us now, and here as it might be when Mr Noakes has done with it. Where there is the familiar pastoral refinement of an Englishman's garden, here is an eruption of gloomy forest and towering crag, of ruins where there was never a house, of water dashing against rocks where there was neither spring nor a stone I could not throw the length of a cricket pitch. My hyacinth dell is become a haunt for hobgoblins, my Chinese bridge, which I am assured is superior to the one at Kew, and for all I know at Peking, is usurped by a fallen obelisk overgrown with briars –

NOAKES: (*Bleating*) Lord Little has one very similar –

LADY CROOM: I cannot relieve Lord Little's misfortunes by adding to my own. Pray, what is this rustic hovel that presumes to superpose itself on my gazebo?

NOAKES: That is the hermitage, madam.

LADY CROOM: I am bewildered.

BRICE: It is all irregular, Mr Noakes.

NOAKES: It is, sir. Irregularity is one of the chiefest principles of the picturesque style –

LADY CROOM: But Sidley Park is already a picture, and a most amiable picture too. The slopes are green and gentle. The trees are companionably grouped at intervals that show them to advantage. The rill is a serpentine ribbon unwound from the lake peaceably contained by meadows on which the right amount of sheep are tastefully arranged – in short, it is nature as God intended, and I can say with the painter, '*Et in Arcadia ego*!' 'Here I am in Arcadia,' Thomasina.

THOMASINA: Yes, mama, if you would have it so.

LADY CROOM: Is she correcting my taste or my translation?

THOMASINA: Neither are beyond correction, mama, but it was your geography caused the doubt.

LADY CROOM: Something has occurred with the girl since I saw her last, and surely that was yesterday. How old are you this morning?

THOMASINA: Thirteen years and ten months, mama.

LADY CROOM: Thirteen years and ten months. She is not due to be pert for six months at the earliest, or to have notions of

taste for much longer. Mr Hodge, I hold you accountable.
Mr Noakes, back to you –

NOAKES: Thank you, my –

LADY CROOM: You have been reading too many novels by Mrs
Radcliffe, that is my opinion. This is a garden for *The Castle
of Otranto* or *The Mysteries of Udolpho* –

CHATER: *The Castle of Otranto*, my lady, is by Horace Walpole.

NOAKES: (*Thrilled*) Mr Walpole the gardener?!

LADY CROOM: Mr Chater, you are a welcome guest at Sidley Park
but while you are one, *The Castle of Otranto* was written by
whomsoever I say it was, otherwise what is the point of being
a guest or having one?
(*The distant popping of guns heard.*)
Well, the guns have reached the brow – I will speak to his
lordship on the subject, and we will see by and by – (*She
stands looking out.*) Ah! – your friend has got down a pigeon,
Mr Hodge. (*Calls out.*) Bravo, sir!

SEPTIMUS: The pigeon, I am sure, fell to your husband or to your
son, your ladyship – my schoolfriend was never a sportsman.

BRICE: (*Looking out*) Yes, to Augustus! – bravo, lad!

LADY CROOM: (*Outside*) Well, come along! Where are my troops?
(*BRICE, NOAKES and CHATER obediently follow her, CHATER
making a detour to shake SEPTIMUS's hand fervently.*)

CHATER: My dear Mr Hodge!
(*CHATER leaves also. The guns are heard again, a little closer.*)

THOMASINA: Pop, pop, pop . . . I have grown up in the sound of
guns like the child of a siege. Pigeons and rooks in the close
season, grouse on the heights from August, and the
pheasants to follow – partridge, snipe, woodcock, and teal –
pop – pop – pop, and the culling of the herd. Papa has no
need of the recording angel, his life is written in the game
book.

SEPTIMUS: A calendar of slaughter. 'Even in Arcadia, there am
I!'

THOMASINA: Oh, phooey to Death!
(*She dips a pen and takes it to the reading stand.*)
I will put in a hermit, for what is a hermitage without a
hermit? Are you in love with my mother, Septimus?

SEPTIMUS: You must not be cleverer than your elders. It is not polite.

THOMASINA: Am I cleverer?

SEPTIMUS: Yes. Much.

THOMASINA: Well, I am sorry, Septimus. (*She pauses in her drawing and produces a small envelope from her pocket.*) Mrs Chater came to the music room with a note for you. She said it was of scant importance, and that therefore I should carry it to you with the utmost safety, urgency and discretion. Does carnal embrace addle the brain?

SEPTIMUS: (*Taking the letter*) Invariably. Thank you. That is enough education for today.

THOMASINA: There. I have made him like the Baptist in the wilderness.

SEPTIMUS: How picturesque.

(LADY CROOM *is heard calling distantly for* THOMASINA *who runs off into the garden, cheerfully, an uncomplicated girl.* SEPTIMUS *opens Mrs Chater's note. He crumples the envelope and throws it away. He reads the note, folds it and inserts it into the pages of 'The Couch of Eros'.*)

SCENE TWO

The lights come up on the same room, on the same sort of morning, in the present day, as is instantly clear from the appearance of HANNAH JARVIS; *and from nothing else.*

Something needs to be said about this. The action of the play shuttles back and forth between the early nineteenth century and the present day, always in this same room. Both periods must share the state of the room, without the additions and subtractions which would normally be expected. The general appearance of the room should offend neither period. In the case of props – books, paper, flowers, etc., there is no absolute need to remove the evidence of one period to make way for another. However, books, etc., used in both periods should exist in both old and new versions. The landscape outside, we are told, has undergone changes. Again, what we see should neither change nor contradict.

On the above principle, the ink and pens etc., of the first scene can remain. Books and papers associated with Hannah's research, in Scene Two, can have been on the table from the beginning of the play. And so on. During the course of the play the table collects this and that, and where an object from one scene would be an anachronism in another (say a coffee mug) it is simply deemed to have become invisible. By the end of the play the table has collected an inventory of objects.

HANNAH *is leafing through the pages of Mr Noakes's sketch book. Also to hand, opened and closed, are a number of small volumes like diaries (these turn out to be Lady Croom's 'garden books'). After a few moments,* HANNAH *takes the sketch book to the windows, comparing the view with what has been drawn, and then she replaces the sketch book on the reading stand.*

She wears nothing frivolous. Her shoes are suitable for the garden, which is where she goes now after picking up the theodolite from the table. The room is empty for a few moments.

One of the other doors opens to admit CHLOË *and* BERNARD. *She is the daughter of the house and is dressed casually.* BERNARD, *the visitor, wears a suit and a tie. His tendency is to dress flamboyantly, but he has damped it down for the occasion, slightly. A peacock-coloured display handkerchief boils over in his breast pocket. He carries a capacious leather bag which serves as a briefcase.*

CHLOË: Oh! Well, she *was* here . . .

BERNARD: Ah . . . the french window . . .

CHLOË: Yes. Hang on.

> (CHLOË *steps out through the garden door and disappears from view.* BERNARD *hangs on. The second door opens and* VALENTINE *looks in.*)

VALENTINE: Sod.

> (VALENTINE *goes out again, closing the door.* CHLOË *returns, carrying a pair of rubber boots. She comes in and sits down and starts exchanging her shoes for the boots, while she talks.*)

CHLOË: The best thing is, you wait here, save you tramping around. She spends a good deal of time in the garden, as you may imagine.

BERNARD: Yes. Why?

CHLOË: Well, she's writing a history of the garden, didn't you know?

BERNARD: No, I knew she was working on the Croom papers but . . .

CHLOË: Well, it's not exactly a history of the garden either. I'll let Hannah explain it. The trench you nearly drove into is all to do with it. I was going to say make yourself comfortable but that's hardly possible, everything's been cleared out, it's en route to the nearest lavatory.

BERNARD: Everything is?

CHLOË: No, this room is. They drew the line at chemical 'Ladies''.

BERNARD: Yes, I see. Did you say Hannah?

CHLOË: Hannah, yes. Will you be all right?

> (*She stands up wearing the boots.*)

I won't be . . . (*But she has lost him.*) Mr Nightingale?

BERNARD: (*Waking up*) Yes. Thank you. Miss Jarvis is Hannah Jarvis the author?

CHLOË: Yes. Have you read her book?

BERNARD: Oh, yes. Yes.

CHLOË: I bet she's in the hermitage, can't see from here with the marquee . . .

BERNARD: Are you having a garden party?

CHLOË: A dance for the district, our annual dressing up and general drunkenness. The wrinklies won't have it in the house, there was a teapot we once had to bag back from Christie's in the nick of time, so anything that can be destroyed, stolen or vomited on has been tactfully removed; tactlessly, I should say –

(*She is about to leave.*)

BERNARD: Um – look – would you tell her – would you mind not mentioning my name just yet?

CHLOË: Oh. All right.

BERNARD: (*Smiling*) More fun to surprise her. Would you mind?

CHLOË: No. But she's bound to ask . . . Should I give you another name, just for the moment?

BERNARD: Yes, why not?

CHLOË: Perhaps another bird, you're not really a Nightingale.

(*She leaves again.* BERNARD *glances over the books on the table. He puts his briefcase down. There is the distant pop-pop of a shotgun. It takes* BERNARD *vaguely to the window. He looks out. The door he entered by now opens and* GUS *looks into the room.* BERNARD *turns and sees him.*)

BERNARD: Hello.

(GUS *doesn't speak. He never speaks. Perhaps he cannot speak. He has no composure, and faced with a stranger, he caves in and leaves again. A moment later the other door opens again and* VALENTINE *crosses the room, not exactly ignoring* BERNARD *and yet ignoring him.*)

VALENTINE: Sod, sod, sod, sod, sod, sod . . . (*As many times as it takes him to leave by the opposite door, which he closes behind him. Beyond it, he can be heard shouting.* Chlo! Chlo! BERNARD's *discomfort increases. The same door opens and* VALENTINE *returns. He looks at* BERNARD.)

BERNARD: She's in the garden looking for Miss Jarvis.

VALENTINE: Where is everything?

BERNARD: It's been removed for the, er . . .

VALENTINE: The dance is all in the tent, isn't it?

BERNARD: Yes, but this is the way to the nearest toilet.

VALENTINE: I need the commode.

BERNARD: Oh. Can't you use the toilet?

VALENTINE: It's got all the game books in it.

BERNARD: Ah. The toilet has or the commode has?

VALENTINE: Is anyone looking after you?

BERNARD: Yes. Thank you. I'm Bernard Nigh— I've come to see Miss Jarvis. I wrote to Lord Croom but unfortunately I never received a reply, so I –

VALENTINE: Did you type it?

BERNARD: Type it?

VALENTINE: Was your letter typewritten?

BERNARD: Yes.

VALENTINE: My father never replies to typewritten letters.
    (*He spots a tortoise which has been half-hidden on the table.*)
    Oh! Where have you been hiding, Lightning? (*He picks up the tortoise.*)

BERNARD: So I telephoned yesterday and I think I spoke to you –

VALENTINE: To me? Ah! Yes! Sorry! You're doing a talk about – someone – and you wanted to ask Hannah – something –

BERNARD: Yes. As it turns out. I'm hoping Miss Jarvis will look kindly on me.

VALENTINE: I doubt it.

BERNARD: Ah, you know about research?

VALENTINE: I know Hannah.

BERNARD: Has she been here long?

VALENTINE: Well in possession, I'm afraid. My mother had read her book, you see. Have you?

BERNARD: No. Yes. Her book. Indeed.

VALENTINE: She's terrifically pleased with herself.

BERNARD: Well, I dare say if I wrote a bestseller –

VALENTINE: No, for reading it. My mother basically reads gardening books.

BERNARD: She must be delighted to have Hannah Jarvis writing a book about her garden.

VALENTINE: Actually it's about hermits.
    (GUS *returns through the same door, and turns to leave again.*)
    It's all right, Gus – what do you want? –
    (*But* GUS *has gone again.*)
    Well . . . I'll take Lightning for his run.

BERNARD: Actually, we've met before. At Sussex, a couple of years ago, a seminar . . .

VALENTINE: Oh. Was I there?

BERNARD: Yes. One of my colleagues believed he had found an unattributed short story by D. H. Lawrence, and he analysed it on his home computer, most interesting, perhaps you remember the paper?

VALENTINE: Not really. But I often sit with my eyes closed and it doesn't necessarily mean I'm awake.

BERNARD: Well, by comparing sentence structures and so forth, this chap showed that there was a ninety per cent chance that the story had indeed been written by the same person as *Women in Love*. To my inexpressible joy, one of your maths mob was able to show that on the same statistical basis there was a ninety per cent chance that Lawrence also wrote the *Just William* books and much of the previous day's *Brighton and Hove Argus*.

VALENTINE: (*Pause*) Oh, Brighton. Yes. I was there. (*And looking out.*) Oh – here she comes, I'll leave you to talk. By the way, is yours the red Mazda?

BERNARD: Yes.

VALENTINE: If you want a tip I'd put it out of sight through the stable arch before my father comes in. He won't have anyone in the house with a Japanese car. Are you queer?

BERNARD: No, actually.

VALENTINE: Well, even so.

(VALENTINE *leaves, closing the door.* BERNARD *keeps staring at the closed door. Behind him,* HANNAH *comes to the garden door.*)

HANNAH: Mr Peacock?

(BERNARD *looks round vaguely then checks over his shoulder for the missing Peacock, then recovers himself and turns on the Nightingale bonhomie.*)

BERNARD: Oh . . . hello! Hello. Miss Jarvis, of course. Such a pleasure. I was thrown for a moment – the photograph doesn't do you justice.

HANNAH: Photograph?

(*Her shoes have got muddy and she is taking them off.*)

BERNARD: On the book. I'm sorry to have brought you indoors, but Lady Chloë kindly insisted she –

HANNAH: No matter – you would have muddied your shoes.

BERNARD: How thoughtful. And how kind of you to spare me a little of your time.

(*He is overdoing it. She shoots him a glance.*)

HANNAH: Are you a journalist?

BERNARD: (*Shocked*) No!

HANNAH: (*Resuming*) I've been in the ha-ha, very squelchy.

BERNARD: (*Unexpectedly*) Ha-*hah*!

HANNAH: What?

BERNARD: A theory of mine. Ha-hah, not ha-ha. If you were strolling down the garden and all of a sudden the ground gave way at your feet, you're not going to go 'ha-ha', you're going to jump back and go 'ha-hah!', or more probably, 'Bloody 'ell!' . . . though personally I think old Murray was up the pole on that one – in France, you know, 'ha-ha' is used to denote a strikingly ugly woman, a much more likely bet for something that keeps the cows off the lawn.

(*This is not going well for* BERNARD *but he seems blithely unaware.*

HANNAH *stares at him for a moment.*)

HANNAH: Mr Peacock, what can I do for you?

BERNARD: Well, to begin with, you can call me Bernard, which is my name.

HANNAH: Thank you.

(*She goes to the garden door to bang her shoes together and scrape off the worst of the mud.*)

BERNARD: The book! – the book is a revelation! To see Caroline Lamb through your eyes is really like seeing her for the first time. I'm ashamed to say I never read her fiction, and how right you are, it's extraordinary stuff – Early Nineteenth is my period as much as anything is.

HANNAH: You teach?

BERNARD: Yes. And write, like you, like we all, though I've never done anything which has sold like *Caro*.

HANNAH: I don't teach.

BERNARD: No. All the more credit to you. To rehabilitate a

forgotten writer, I suppose you could say that's the main reason for an English don.

HANNAH: Not to teach?

BERNARD: Good God, no, let the brats sort it out for themselves. Anyway, many congratulations. I expect someone will be bringing out Caroline Lamb's oeuvre now?

HANNAH: Yes, I expect so.

BERNARD: How wonderful! Bravo! Simply as a document shedding reflected light on the character of Lord Byron, it's bound to be –

HANNAH: Bernard. You did say Bernard, didn't you?

BERNARD: I did.

HANNAH: I'm putting my shoes on again.

BERNARD: Oh. You're not going to go out?

HANNAH: No, I'm going to kick you in the balls.

BERNARD: Right. Point taken. Ezra Chater.

HANNAH: Ezra Chater.

BERNARD: Born Twickenham, Middlesex, 1778, author of two verse narratives, 'The Maid of Turkey', 1808, and 'The Couch of Eros', 1809. Nothing known after 1809, disappears from view.

HANNAH: I see. And?

BERNARD: (*Reaching for his bag*) There is a Sidley Park connection.

(*He produces 'The Couch of Eros' from the bag. He reads the inscription.*)

'To my friend Septimus Hodge, who stood up and gave his best on behalf of the Author – Ezra Chater, at Sidley Park, Derbyshire, April 10th 1809.

(*He gives her the book.*)

I am in your hands.

HANNAH: 'The Couch of Eros'. Is it any good?

BERNARD: Quite surprising.

HANNAH: You think there's a book in him?

BERNARD: No, no – a monograph perhaps for the *Journal of English Studies*. There's almost nothing on Chater, not a word in the *DNB*, of course – by that time he'd been completely forgotten.

HANNAH: Family?

BERNARD: Zilch. There's only one other Chater in the British Library database.

HANNAH: Same period?

BERNARD: Yes, but he wasn't a poet like our Ezra, he was a botanist who described a dwarf dahlia in Martinique and died there after being bitten by a monkey.

HANNAH: And Ezra Chater?

BERNARD: He gets two references in the periodical index, one for each book, in both cases a substantial review in the *Piccadilly Recreation*, a thrice weekly folio sheet, but giving no personal details.

HANNAH: And where was this (*the book*)?

BERNARD: Private collection. I've got a talk to give next week, in London, and I think Chater is interesting, so anything on him, or this Septimus Hodge, Sidley Park, any leads at all . . . I'd be most grateful.

(*Pause.*)

HANNAH: Well! This is a new experience for me. A grovelling academic.

BERNARD: Oh, I say.

HANNAH: Oh, but it is. All the academics who reviewed my book patronized it.

BERNARD: Surely not.

HANNAH: Surely yes. The Byron gang unzipped their flies and patronized all over it. Where is it you don't bother to teach, by the way?

BERNARD: Oh, well, Sussex, actually.

HANNAH: Sussex. (*She thinks a moment.*) Nightingale. Yes; a thousand words in the *Observer* to see me off the premises with a pat on the bottom. You must know him.

BERNARD: As I say, I'm in your hands.

HANNAH: Quite. Say please, then.

BERNARD: Please.

HANNAH: Sit down, do.

BERNARD: Thank you.

(*He takes a chair. She remains standing. Possibly she smokes; if so, perhaps now. A short cigarette-holder sounds right, too. Or brown-paper cigarillos.*)

HANNAH: How did you know I was here?

BERNARD: Oh, I didn't. I spoke to the son on the phone but he didn't mention you by name . . . and then he forgot to mention me.

HANNAH: Valentine. He's at Oxford, technically.

BERNARD: Yes, I met him. Brideshead Regurgitated.

HANNAH: My fiancé.

(*She holds his look.*)

BERNARD: (*Pause*) I'll take a chance. You're lying.

HANNAH: (*Pause*) Well done, Bernard.

BERNARD: Christ.

HANNAH: He calls me his fiancée.

BERNARD: Why?

HANNAH: It's a joke.

BERNARD: You turned him down?

HANNAH: Don't be silly, do I look like the next Countess of –

BERNARD: No, no – a freebie. The joke that consoles. My tortoise Lightning, my fiancée Hannah.

HANNAH: Oh. Yes. You have a way with you, Bernard. I'm not sure I like it.

BERNARD: What's he doing, Valentine?

HANNAH: He's a postgrad. Biology.

BERNARD: No, he's a mathematician.

HANNAH: Well, he's doing grouse.

BERNARD: Grouse?

HANNAH: Not actual grouse. Computer grouse.

BERNARD: Who's the one who doesn't speak?

HANNAH: Gus.

BERNARD: What's the matter with him?

HANNAH: I didn't ask.

BERNARD: And the father sounds like a lot of fun.

HANNAH: Ah yes.

BERNARD: And the mother is the gardener. What's going on here?

HANNAH: What do you mean?

BERNARD: I nearly took her head off – she was standing in a trench at the time.

HANNAH: Archaeology. The house had a formal Italian garden

until about 1740. Lady Croom is interested in garden history. I sent her my book – it contains, as you know if you've read it – which I'm not assuming, by the way – a rather good description of Caroline's garden at Brocket Hall. I'm here now helping Hermione.

BERNARD: (*Impressed*) Hermione.

HANNAH: The records are unusually complete and they have never been worked on.

BERNARD: I'm beginning to admire you.

HANNAH: Before was bullshit?

BERNARD: Completely. Your photograph does you justice, I'm not sure the book does.
(*She considers him. He waits, confident.*)

HANNAH: Septimus Hodge was the tutor.

BERNARD: (*Quietly*) Attagirl.

HANNAH: His pupil was the Croom daughter. There was a son at Eton. Septimus lived in the house: the pay book specifies allowances for wine and candles. So, not quite a guest but rather more than a steward. His letter of self-recommendation is preserved among the papers. I'll dig it out for you. As far as I remember he studied mathematics and natural philosophy at Cambridge. A scientist, therefore, as much as anything.

BERNARD: I'm impressed. Thank you. And Chater?

HANNAH: Nothing.

BERNARD: Oh. Nothing at all?

HANNAH: I'm afraid not.

BERNARD: How about the library?

HANNAH: The catalogue was done in the 1880s. I've been through the lot.

BERNARD: Books or catalogue?

HANNAH: Catalogue.

BERNARD: Ah. Pity.

HANNAH: I'm sorry.

BERNARD: What about the letters? No mention?

HANNAH: I'm afraid not. I've been very thorough in your period because, of course, it's my period too.

BERNARD: Is it? Actually, I don't quite know what it is you're . . .

24

HANNAH: The Sidley hermit.

BERNARD: Ah. Who's he?

HANNAH: He's my peg for the nervous breakdown of the Romantic Imagination. I'm doing landscape and literature 1750 to 1834.

BERNARD: What happened in 1834?

HANNAH: My hermit died.

BERNARD: Of course.

HANNAH: What do you mean, of course?

BERNARD: Nothing.

HANNAH: Yes, you do.

BERNARD: No, no . . . However, Coleridge also died in 1834.

HANNAH: So he did. What a stroke of luck. (*Softening.*) Thank you, Bernard.
(*She goes to the reading stand and opens Noakes's sketch book.*)
Look – there he is.
(BERNARD *goes to look.*)

BERNARD: Mmm.

HANNAH: The only known likeness of the Sidley hermit.

BERNARD: Very biblical.

HANNAH: Drawn in by a later hand, of course. The hermitage didn't yet exist when Noakes did the drawings.

BERNARD: Noakes . . . the painter?

HANNAH: Landscape gardener. He'd do these books for his clients, as a sort of prospectus. (*She demonstrates.*) Before and after, you see. This is how it all looked until, say, 1810 – smooth, undulating, serpentine – open water, clumps of trees, classical boat-house –

BERNARD: Lovely. The real England.

HANNAH: You can stop being silly now, Bernard. English landscape was invented by gardeners imitating foreign painters who were evoking classical authors. The whole thing was brought home in the luggage from the grand tour. Here, look – Capability Brown doing Claude, who was doing Virgil. Arcadia! And here, superimposed by Richard Noakes, untamed nature in the style of Salvator Rosa. It's the Gothic novel expressed in landscape. Everything but vampires. There's an account of my hermit in a letter by your illustrious namesake.

25

BERNARD: Florence?

HANNAH: What?

BERNARD: No. You go on.

HANNAH: Thomas Love Peacock.

BERNARD: Ah yes.

HANNAH: I found it in an essay on hermits and anchorites published in the *Cornhill Magazine* in the 1860s . . . (*She fishes for the magazine itself among the books on the table, and finds it.*) . . . 1862 . . . Peacock calls him (*She quotes from memory.*) 'Not one of your village simpletons to frighten the ladies, but a savant among idiots, a sage of lunacy.'

BERNARD: An oxy-moron, so to speak.

HANNAH: (*Busy*) Yes. What?

BERNARD: Nothing.

HANNAH: (*Having found the place*) Here we are. 'A letter we have seen, written by the author of *Headlong Hall* nearly thirty years ago, tells of a visit to the Earl of Croom's estate, Sidley Park – '

BERNARD: Was the letter to Thackeray?

HANNAH: (*Brought up short*) I don't know. Does it matter?

BERNARD: No. Sorry.

(*But the gaps he leaves for her are false promises – and she is not quick enough. That's how it goes.*)

Only, Thackeray edited the *Cornhill* until '63 when, as you know, he died. His father had been with the East India Company where Peacock, of course, had held the position of Examiner, so it's quite possible that if the essay were by Thackeray, the *letter* . . . Sorry. Go on.

Of course, the East India Library in Blackfriars has most of Peacock's letters, so it would be quite easy to . . . Sorry. Can I look?

(*Silently she hands him the* Cornhill.)

Yes, it's been topped and tailed, of course. It might be worth . . . Go on. I'm listening . . .

(*Leafing through the essay, he suddenly chuckles.*) Oh yes, it's Thackeray all right . . .

(*He slaps the book shut.*) Unbearable . . .

(*He hands it back to her.*) What were you saying?

HANNAH: Are you always like this?

BERNARD: Like what?

HANNAH: The point is, the Crooms, of course, had the hermit under their noses for twenty years so hardly thought him worth remarking. As I'm finding out. The Peacock letter is still the main source, unfortunately. When I read this (*the magazine in her hand*) well, it was one of those moments that tell you what your next book is going to be. The hermit of Sidley Park was my . . .

BERNARD: Peg.

HANNAH: Epiphany.

BERNARD: Epiphany, that's it.

HANNAH: The hermit was *placed* in the landscape exactly as one might place a pottery gnome. And there he lived out his life as a garden ornament.

BERNARD: Did he do anything?

HANNAH: Oh, he was very busy. When he died, the cottage was stacked solid with paper. Hundreds of pages. Thousands. Peacock says he was suspected of genius. It turned out, of course, he was off his head. He'd covered every sheet with cabalistic proofs that the world was coming to an end. It's perfect, isn't it? A perfect symbol, I mean.

BERNARD: Oh, yes. Of what?

HANNAH: The whole Romantic sham, Bernard! It's what happened to the Enlightenment, isn't it? A century of intellectual rigour turned in on itself. A mind in chaos suspected of genius. In a setting of cheap thrills and false emotion. The history of the garden says it all, beautifully. There's an engraving of Sidley Park in 1730 that makes you want to weep. Paradise in the age of reason. By 1760 everything had gone – the topiary, pools and terraces, fountains, an avenue of limes – the whole sublime geometry was ploughed under by Capability Brown. The grass went from the doorstep to the horizon and the best box hedge in Derbyshire was dug up for the ha-ha so that the fools could pretend they were living in God's countryside. And then Richard Noakes came in to bring God up to date. By the time he'd finished it looked like this (*the sketch book*). The decline from thinking to feeling, you see.

27

BERNARD: (*A judgement*) That's awfully good.

    (HANNAH *looks at him in case of irony but he is professional*.)

    No, that'll stand up.

HANNAH: Thank you.

BERNARD: Personally I like the ha-ha. Do you like hedges?

HANNAH: I don't like sentimentality.

BERNARD: Yes, I see. Are you sure? You seem quite sentimental over geometry. But the hermit is very very good. The genius of the place.

HANNAH: (*Pleased*) That's my title!

BERNARD: Of course.

HANNAH: (*Less pleased*) Of course?

BERNARD: Of course. Who was he when he wasn't being a symbol?

HANNAH: I don't know.

BERNARD: Ah.

HANNAH: I mean, yet.

BERNARD: Absolutely. What did they do with all the paper? Does Peacock say?

HANNAH: Made a bonfire.

BERNARD: Ah, well.

HANNAH: I've still got Lady Croom's garden books to go through.

BERNARD: Account books or journals?

HANNAH: A bit of both. They're gappy but they span the period.

HANNAH: Really? Have you come across Byron at all? As a matter of interest.

HANNAH: A first edition of 'Childe Harold' in the library, and *English Bards*, I think.

BERNARD: Inscribed?

HANNAH: No.

BERNARD: And he doesn't pop up in the letters at all?

HANNAH: Why should he? The Crooms don't pop up in his.

BERNARD: (*Casually*) That's true, of course. But Newstead isn't so far away. Would you mind terribly if I poked about a bit? Only in the papers you've done with, of course.

    (HANNAH *twigs something*.)

HANNAH: Are you looking into Byron or Chater?
  (CHLOË *enters in stockinged feet through one of the side doors,
  laden with an armful of generally similar leather-covered ledgers.
  She detours to collect her shoes.*)
CHLOË: Sorry – just cutting through – there's tea in the pantry if
  you don't mind mugs –
BERNARD: How kind.
CHLOË: Hannah will show you.
BERNARD: Let me help you.
CHLOË: No, it's all right –
  (BERNARD *opens the opposite door for her.*)
  Thank you – I've been saving Val's game books. Thanks.
  (BERNARD *closes the door.*)
BERNARD: Sweet girl.
HANNAH: Mmm.
BERNARD: Oh, really?
HANNAH: Oh really what?
  (CHLOË*'s door opens again and she puts her head round it.*)
CHLOË: Meant to say, don't worry if father makes remarks about
  your car, Mr Nightingale, he's got a thing about – (*and the
  Nightingale now being out of the bag*) ooh – ah, how was the
  surprise? – not yet, eh? Oh, well – sorry – tea, anyway – so
  sorry if I – (*Embarrassed, she leaves again, closing the door.
  Pause.*)
HANNAH: You absolute shit.
  (*She heads off to leave.*)
BERNARD: The thing is, there's a Byron connection too.
  (HANNAH *stops and faces him.*)
HANNAH: I don't care.
BERNARD: You should. The Byron gang are going to get their
  dicks caught in their zip.
HANNAH: (*Pause*) Oh really?
BERNARD: If we collaborate.
HANNAH: On what?
BERNARD: Sit down, I'll tell you.
HANNAH: I'll stand for the moment.
BERNARD: This copy of 'The Couch of Eros' belonged to Lord
  Byron.

HANNAH: It belonged to Septimus Hodge.

BERNARD: Originally, yes. But it was in Byron's library which was sold to pay his debts when he left England for good in 1816. The sales catalogue is in the British Library. 'Eros' was lot 74A and was bought by the bookseller and publisher John Nightingale of Opera Court, Pall Mall . . . whose name survives in the firm of Nightingale and Matlock, the present Nightingale being my cousin.

(*He pauses.* HANNAH *hesitates and then sits down at the table.*)

I'll just give you the headlines. 1939, stock removed to Nightingale country house in Kent. 1945, stock returned to bookshop. Meanwhile, overlooked box of early nineteenth-century books languish in country house cellar until house sold to make way for the Channel Tunnel rail-link. 'Eros' discovered with sales slip from 1816 attached – photocopy available for inspection.

(*He brings this from his bag and gives it to* HANNAH *who inspects it.*)

HANNAH: All right. It was in Byron's library.

BERNARD: A number of passages have been underlined.

(HANNAH *picks up the book and leafs through it.*)

All of them, and only them – no, no, look at me, not at the book – all the underlined passages, word for word, were used as quotations in the review of 'The Couch of Eros' in the *Piccadilly Recreation* of April 30th 1809. The reviewer begins by drawing attention to his previous notice in the same periodical of 'The Maid of Turkey'.

HANNAH: The reviewer is obviously Hodge. 'My friend Septimus Hodge who stood up and gave his best on behalf of the Author.'

BERNARD: That's the point. The *Piccadilly* ridiculed both books.

HANNAH: (*Pause.*) Do the reviews read like Byron?

BERNARD: (*Producing two photocopies from his case*) They read a damn sight more like Byron than Byron's review of Wordsworth the previous year.

(HANNAH *glances over the photocopies.*)

HANNAH: I see. Well, congratulations. Possibly. Two previously unknown book reviews by the young Byron. Is that it?

BERNARD: No. Because of the tapes, three documents survived undisturbed in the book.

(He has been carefully opening a package produced from his bag. He has the originals. He holds them carefully one by one.)

'Sir – we have a matter to settle. I wait on you in the gun room. E. Chater, Esq.'

'My husband has sent to town for pistols. Deny what cannot be proven – for Charity's sake – I keep my room this day.' Unsigned.

'Sidley Park, April 11th 1809. Sir – I call you a liar, a lecher, a slanderer in the press and a thief of my honour. I wait upon your arrangements for giving me satisfaction as a man and a poet. E. Chater, Esq.'

(Pause.)

HANNAH: Superb. But inconclusive. The book had seven years to find its way into Byron's possession. It doesn't connect Byron with Chater, or with Sidley Park. Or with Hodge for that matter. Furthermore, there isn't a hint in Byron's letters and this kind of scrape is the last thing he would have kept quiet about.

BERNARD: *Scrape?*

HANNAH: He would have made a comic turn out of it.

BERNARD: Comic turn, fiddlesticks! *(He pauses for effect.)* He killed Chater!

HANNAH: *(A raspberry)* Oh, really!

BERNARD: Chater was thirty-one years old. The author of two books. Nothing more is heard from him after 'Eros'. He disappears completely after April 1809. And Byron – Byron had just published his satire, *English Bards and Scotch Reviewers,* in March. He was just getting a name. Yet he sailed for Lisbon as soon as he could find a ship, and stayed abroad for two years. Hannah, *this is fame.* Somewhere in the Croom papers there will be *something –*

HANNAH: There isn't, I've looked.

BERNARD: But you were looking for something else! It's not

going to jump out at you like 'Lord Byron remarked wittily at breakfast!'

HANNAH: Nevertheless his presence would be unlikely to have gone unremarked. But there is nothing to suggest that Byron was here, and I don't believe he ever was.

BERNARD: All right, but let me have a look.

HANNAH: You'll queer my pitch.

BERNARD: Dear girl, I know how to handle myself –

HANNAH: And don't call me dear girl. If I find anything on Byron, or Chater, or Hodge, I'll pass it on. Nightingale, Sussex.

(*Pause. She stands up.*)

BERNARD: Thank you. I'm sorry about that business with my name.

HANNAH: Don't mention it . . .

BERNARD: What was Hodge's college, by the way?

HANNAH: Trinity.

BERNARD: Trinity?

HANNAH: Yes. (*She hesitates.*) Yes. Byron's old college.

BERNARD: How old was Hodge?

HANNAH: I'd have to look it up but a year or two older than Byron. Twenty-two . . .

BERNARD: Contemporaries at Trinity?

HANNAH: (*Wearily*) Yes, Bernard, and no doubt they were both in the cricket eleven when Harrow played Eton at Lords!

(BERNARD *approaches her and stands close to her.*)

BERNARD: (*Evenly*) Do you mean that Septimus Hodge was at school with Byron?

HANNAH: (*Falters slightly*) Yes . . . he must have been . . . as a matter of fact.

BERNARD: Well, you silly cow.

(*With a large gesture of pure happiness,* BERNARD *throws his arms around* HANNAH *and gives her a great smacking kiss on the cheek.* CHLOË *enters to witness the end of this.*)

CHLOË: Oh – erm . . . I thought I'd bring it to you.

(*She is carrying a small tray with two mugs on it.*)

BERNARD: I have to go and see about my car.

HANNAH: Going to hide it?

BERNARD: Hide it? I'm going to sell it! Is there a pub I can put up
at in the village?
(*He turns back to them as he is about to leave through the
garden.*)
Aren't you glad I'm here?
(*He leaves.*)

CHLOË: He said he knew you.

HANNAH: He couldn't have.

CHLOË: No, perhaps not. He said he wanted to be a surprise, but
I suppose that's different. I thought there was a lot of sexual
energy there, didn't you?

HANNAH: What?

CHLOË: Bouncy on his feet, you see, a sure sign. Should I invite
him for you?

HANNAH: To what? No.

CHLOË: You can invite him – that's better. He can come as your
partner.

HANNAH: Stop it. Thank you for the tea.

CHLOË: If you don't want him, I'll have him. Is he married?

HANNAH: I haven't the slightest idea. Aren't you supposed to
have a pony?

CHLOË: I'm just trying to fix you up, Hannah.

HANNAH: Believe me, it gets less important.

CHLOË: I mean for the dancing. He can come as Beau Brummel.

HANNAH: I don't want to dress up and I don't want a dancing
partner, least of all Mr Nightingale. I don't dance.

CHLOË: Don't be such a prune. You were kissing him, anyway.

HANNAH: He was kissing me, and only out of general enthusiasm.

CHLOË: Well, don't say I didn't give you first chance. My genius
brother will be much relieved. He's in love with you, I
suppose you know.

HANNAH: (*Angry*) That's a joke!

CHLOË: It's not a joke to him.

HANNAH: Of course it is – not even a joke – how can you be so
ridiculous?
(GUS *enters from the garden, in his customary silent
awkwardness.*)

CHLOË: Hello, Gus, what have you got?

(GUS *has an apple, just picked, with a leaf or two still attached.*
He offers the apple to HANNAH.)
HANNAH: (*Surprised*) Oh! . . . Thank you!
CHLOË: (*Leaving*) Told you.
(CHLOË *closes the door on herself.*)
HANNAH: Thank you. Oh dear.

The schoolroom. The next morning. Present are: THOMASINA,
SEPTIMUS, JELLABY. *We have seen this composition before:*
THOMASINA *at her place at the table;* SEPTIMUS *reading a letter which
has just arrived;* JELLABY *waiting, having just delivered the letter.*
    'The Couch of Eros' is in front of SEPTIMUS, *open, together with
sheets of paper on which he has been writing. His portfolio is on the
table. Plautus (the tortoise) is the paperweight. There is also an apple on
the table now, the same apple from all appearances.*

SEPTIMUS: (*With his eyes on the letter*) Why have you stopped?
    (THOMASINA *is studying a sheet of paper, a 'Latin unseen' lesson.
    She is having some difficulty.*)
THOMASINA: *Solio insessa . . . in igne . . .* seated on a throne . . . in
    the fire . . . and also on a ship . . . *sedebat regina . . .* sat the
    queen . . .
SEPTIMUS: There is no reply, Jellaby. Thank you.
    (*He folds the letter up and places it between the leaves of 'The
    Couch of Eros'.*)
JELLABY: I will say so, sir.
THOMASINA: . . . the wind smelling sweetly . . . *purpureis velis . . .*
    by, with or from purple sails –
SEPTIMUS: (*To* JELLABY) I will have something for the post, if you
    would be so kind.
JELLABY: (*Leaving*) Yes, sir.
THOMASINA: . . . was like as to – something – by, with or from
    lovers – oh, Septimus! – *musica tibiarum imperabat . . .* music
    of pipes commanded . . .
SEPTIMUS: 'Ruled' is better.
THOMASINA: . . . the silver oars – exciting the ocean – as if – as if –
    amorous –
SEPTIMUS: That is very good.
    (*He picks up the apple. He picks off the twig and leaves, placing
    these on the table. With a pocket knife he cuts a slice of apple, and
    while he eats it, cuts another slice which he offers to Plautus.*)
THOMASINA: *Regina reclinabat . . .* the queen – was reclining –

35

praeter descriptionem – indescribably – in a golden tent . . .
like Venus and yet more –

SEPTIMUS: Try to put some poetry into it.

THOMASINA: How can I if there is none in the Latin?

SEPTIMUS: Oh, a critic!

THOMASINA: Is it Queen Dido?

SEPTIMUS: No.

THOMASINA: Who is the poet?

SEPTIMUS: Known to you.

THOMASINA: Known to me?

SEPTIMUS: Not a Roman.

THOMASINA: Mr Chater?

SEPTIMUS: Your translation is quite like Chater.

(SEPTIMUS *picks up his pen and continues with his own
writing.*)

THOMASINA: I know who it is, it is your friend Byron.

SEPTIMUS: Lord Byron, if you please.

THOMASINA: Mama is in love with Lord Byron.

SEPTIMUS: (*Absorbed*) Yes. Nonsense.

THOMASINA: It is not nonsense. I saw them together in the
gazebo.

(SEPTIMUS's *pen stops moving, he raises his eyes to her at last.*)
Lord Byron was reading to her from his satire, and mama
was laughing, with her head in her best position.

SEPTIMUS: She did not understand the satire, and was showing
politeness to a guest.

THOMASINA: She is vexed with papa for his determination to alter
the park, but that alone cannot account for her politeness to a
guest. She came downstairs hours before her custom. Lord
Byron was amusing at breakfast. He paid you a tribute,
Septimus.

SEPTIMUS: Did he?

THOMASINA: He said you were a witty fellow, and he had almost
by heart an article you wrote about – well, I forget what, but
it concerned a book called 'The Maid of Turkey' and how
you would not give it to your dog for dinner.

SEPTIMUS: Ah. Mr Chater was at breakfast, of course.

THOMASINA: He was, not like certain lazybones.

SEPTIMUS: He does not have Latin to set and mathematics to correct.

(*He takes Thomasina's lesson book from underneath Plautus and tosses it down the table to her.*)

THOMASINA: Correct? What was incorrect in it? (*She looks into the book.*) Alpha minus? Pooh! What is the minus for?

SEPTIMUS: For doing more than was asked.

THOMASINA: You did not like my discovery?

SEPTIMUS: A fancy is not a discovery.

THOMASINA: A gibe is not a rebuttal.

(SEPTIMUS *finishes what he is writing. He folds the pages into a letter. He has sealing wax and the means to melt it. He seals the letter and writes on the cover. Meanwhile –*)

You are churlish with me because mama is paying attention to your friend. Well, let them elope, they cannot turn back the advancement of knowledge. I think it is an excellent discovery. Each week I plot your equations dot for dot, *x*s against *y*s in all manner of algebraical relation, and every week they draw themselves as commonplace geometry, as if the world of forms were nothing but arcs and angles. God's truth, Septimus, if there is an equation for a curve like a bell, there must be an equation for one like a bluebell, and if a bluebell, why not a rose? Do we believe nature is written in numbers?

SEPTIMUS: We do.

THOMASINA: Then why do your equations only describe the shapes of manufacture?

SEPTIMUS: I do not know.

THOMASINA: Armed thus, God could only make a cabinet.

SEPTIMUS: He has mastery of equations which lead into infinities where we cannot follow.

THOMASINA: What a faint-heart! We must work outward from the middle of the maze. We will start with something simple. (*She picks up the apple leaf.*) I will plot this leaf and deduce its equation. You will be famous for being my tutor when Lord Byron is dead and forgotten.

(SEPTIMUS *completes the business with his letter. He puts the letter in his pocket.*)

SEPTIMUS: (*Firmly*) Back to Cleopatra.

THOMASINA: Is it Cleopatra? – I hate Cleopatra!

SEPTIMUS: You hate her? Why?

THOMASINA: Everything is turned to love with her. New love,
absent love, lost love – I never knew a heroine that makes
such noodles of our sex. It only needs a Roman general to
drop anchor outside the window and away goes the empire
like a christening mug into a pawn shop. If Queen Elizabeth
had been a Ptolemy history would have been quite different –
we would be admiring the pyramids of Rome and the great
Sphinx of Verona.

SEPTIMUS: God save us.

THOMASINA: But instead, the Egyptian noodle made carnal
embrace with the enemy who burned the great library of
Alexandria without so much as a fine for all that is overdue.
Oh, Septimus! – can you bear it? All the lost plays of the
Athenians! Two hundred at least by Aeschylus, Sophocles,
Euripides – thousands of poems – Aristotle's own library
brought to Egypt by the noodle's ancestors! How can we
sleep for grief?

SEPTIMUS: By counting our stock. Seven plays from Aeschylus,
seven from Sopocles, *nineteen* from Euripides, my lady! You
should no more grieve for the rest than for a buckle lost from
your first shoe, or for your lesson book which will be lost
when you are old. We shed as we pick up, like travellers who
must carry everything in their arms, and what we let fall will
be picked up by those behind. The procession is very long
and life is very short. We die on the march. But there is
nothing outside the march so nothing can be lost to it. The
missing plays of Sophocles will turn up piece by piece, or be
written again in another language. Ancient cures for diseases
will reveal themselves once more. Mathematical discoveries
glimpsed and lost to view will have their time again. You do
not suppose, my lady, that if all of Archimedes had been
hiding in the great library of Alexandria, we would be at a
loss for a corkscrew? I have no doubt that the improved
steam-driven heat-engine which puts Mr Noakes into an
ecstasy that he and it and the modern age should all coincide,

was described on papyrus. Steam and brass were not invented in Glasgow. Now, where are we? Let me see if I can attempt a free translation for you. At Harrow I was better at this than Lord Byron.

(*He takes the piece of paper from her and scrutinizes it, testing one or two Latin phrases speculatively before committing himself.*)

Yes – 'The barge she sat in, like a burnished throne . . . burned on the water . . . the – something – the poop was beaten gold, purple the sails, and – what's this? – oh yes, – so perfumed that –

THOMASINA: (*Catching on and furious*) Cheat!

SEPTIMUS: (*Imperturbably*) '– the winds were lovesick with them . . .'

THOMASINA: Cheat!

SEPTIMUS: '. . . the oars were silver which to the tune of flutes kept stroke . . .'

THOMASINA: (*Jumping to her feet*) Cheat! Cheat! Cheat!

SEPTIMUS: (*As though it were too easy to make the effort worthwhile*) '. . . and made the water which they beat to follow faster, as *amorous* of their strokes. For her own person, it beggared all description – she did lie in her pavilion –'

(THOMASINA, *in tears of rage, is hurrying out through the garden.*)

THOMASINA: I hope you die!

(*She nearly bumps into* BRICE *who is entering. She runs out of sight.* BRICE *enters.*)

BRICE: Good God, man, what have you told her?

SEPTIMUS: Told her? Told her what?

BRICE: Hodge!

(SEPTIMUS *looks outside the door, slightly contrite about* THOMASINA, *and sees that* CHATER *is skulking out of view.*)

SEPTIMUS: Chater! My dear fellow! Don't hang back – come in, sir!

(CHATER *allows himself to be drawn sheepishly into the room, where* BRICE *stands on his dignity.*)

CHATER: Captain Brice does me the honour – I mean to say, sir, whatever you have to say to me, sir, address yourself to Captain Brice.

SEPTIMUS: How unusual. (*To* BRICE) Your wife did not appear yesterday, sir. I trust she is not sick?

BRICE: My wife? I have no wife. What the devil do you mean, sir? (SEPTIMUS *makes to reply, but hesitates, puzzled. He turns back to* CHATER.)

SEPTIMUS: I do not understand the scheme, Chater. Whom do I address when I want to speak to Captain Brice?

BRICE: Oh, slippery, Hodge – slippery!

SEPTIMUS: (*To* CHATER) By the way, Chater – (*he interrupts himself and turns back to* BRICE, *and continues as before*) by the way, Chater, I have amazing news to tell you. Someone has taken to writing wild and whirling letters in your name. I received one not half an hour ago.

BRICE: (*Angrily*) Mr Hodge! Look to your honour, sir! If you cannot attend to me without this foolery, nominate your second who might settle the business as between gentlemen. No doubt your friend Byron would do you the service. (SEPTIMUS *gives up the game.*)

SEPTIMUS: Oh yes, he would do me the service. (*His mood changes, he turns to* CHATER.) Sir – I repent your injury. You are an honest fellow with no more malice in you than poetry.

CHATER: (*Happily*) Ah well! – that is more like the thing! (*Overtaken by doubt.*) Is he apologizing?

BRICE: There is still the injury to his conjugal property, Mrs Chater's –

CHATER: Tush, sir!

BRICE: As you will – her tush. Nevertheless – (*But they are interrupted by* LADY CROOM, *also entering from the garden.*)

LADY CROOM: Oh – excellently found! Mr Chater, this will please you very much. Lord Byron begs a copy of your new book. He dies to read it and intends to include your name in the second edition of his *English Bards and Scotch Reviewers*.

CHATER: *English Bards and Scotch Reviewers*, your ladyship, is a doggerel aimed at Lord Byron's seniors and betters. If he intends to include me, he intends to insult me.

LADY CROOM: Well, of course he does, Mr Chater. Would you rather be thought not worth insulting? You should be proud

40

to be in the company of Rogers and Moore and Wordsworth—
ah! 'The Couch of Eros!' (*For she has spotted Septimus's copy of the book on the table.*)

SEPTIMUS: That is my copy, madam.

LADY CROOM: So much the better—what are a friend's books for if not to be borrowed?

(*Note: 'The Couch of Eros' now contains the three letters, and it must do so without advertising the fact. This is why the volume has been described as a substantial quarto.*)

Mr Hodge, you must speak to your friend and put him out of his affectation of pretending to quit us. I will not have it. He says he is determined on the Malta packet sailing out of Falmouth! His head is full of Lisbon and Lesbos, and his portmanteau of pistols, and I have told him it is not to be thought of. The whole of Europe is in a Napoleonic fit, all the best ruins will be closed, the roads entirely occupied with the movement of armies, the lodgings turned to billets and the fashion for godless republicanism not yet arrived at its natural reversion. He says his aim is poetry. One does not aim at poetry with pistols. At poets, perhaps. I charge you to take command of his pistols, Mr Hodge! He is not safe with them. His lameness, he confessed to me, is entirely the result of his habit from boyhood of shooting himself in the foot. What is that *noise*?

(*The noise is a badly played piano in the next room. It has been going on for some time since* THOMASINA *left.*)

SEPTIMUS: The new Broadwood pianoforte, madam. Our music lessons are at an early stage.

LADY CROOM: Well, restrict your lessons to the *piano* side of the instrument and let her loose on the *forte* when she has learned something.

(LADY CROOM, *holding the book, sails out back into the garden.*)

BRICE: Now! If that was not God speaking through Lady Croom, he never spoke through anyone!

CHATER: (*Awed*) Take command of Lord Byron's pistols!

BRICE: You hear Mr Chater, sir—how will you answer him?

(SEPTIMUS *has been watching* LADY CROOM's *progress up the garden. He turns back.*)

SEPTIMUS: By killing him. I am tired of him.

CHATER: (*Startled*) Eh?

BRICE: (*Pleased*) Ah!

SEPTIMUS: Oh, damn your soul, Chater! Ovid would have stayed a lawyer and Virgil a farmer if they had known the bathos to which love would descend in your sportive satyrs and noodle nymphs! I am at your service with a half-ounce ball in your brain. May it satisfy you – behind the boat-house at daybreak – shall we say five o'clock? My compliments to Mrs Chater – have no fear for her, she will not want for protection while Captain Brice has a guinea in his pocket, he told her so himself.

BRICE: You lie, sir!

SEPTIMUS: No, sir. Mrs Chater, perhaps.

BRICE: You lie, or you will answer to me!

SEPTIMUS: (*Wearily*) Oh, very well – I can fit you in at five minutes after five. And then it's off to the Malta packet out of Falmouth. You two will be dead, my penurious schoolfriend will remain to tutor Lady Thomasina, and I trust everybody including Lady Croom will be satisfied!

(SEPTIMUS *slams the door behind him.*)

BRICE: He is all bluster and bladder. Rest assured, Chater, I will let the air out of him.

(BRICE *leaves by the other door.* CHATER's *assurance lasts only a moment. When he spots the flaw . . .*

CHATER: Oh! But . . .

(*He hurries out after* BRICE.)

HANNAH *and* VALENTINE. *She is reading aloud. He is listening.*
Lightning, the tortoise, is on the table and is not readily distinguishable
from Plautus. In front of VALENTINE *is Septimus's portfolio,*
recognizably so but naturally somewhat faded. It is open. Principally
associated with the portfolio (although it may contain sheets of blank
paper also) are three items: a slim maths primer; a sheet of drawing
paper on which there is a scrawled diagram and some mathematical
notations, arrow marks, etc.; and Thomasina's mathematics lesson
book, i.e. the one she writes in, which VALENTINE *is leafing through as*
he listens to HANNAH *reading from the primer.*

HANNAH: 'I, Thomasina Coverly, have found a truly wonderful
method whereby all the forms of nature must give up their
numerical secrets and draw themselves through number
alone. This margin being too mean for my purpose, the reader
must look elsewhere for the New Geometry of Irregular
Forms discovered by Thomasina Coverly.'
(Pause. She hands VALENTINE *the text book.* VALENTINE *looks*
at what she has been reading.
From the next room, a piano is heard, beginning to play quietly,
unintrusively, improvisationally.)
Does it mean anything?

VALENTINE: I don't know. I don't know what it means, except
mathematically.

HANNAH: I meant mathematically.

VALENTINE: (*Now with the lesson book again*) It's an iterated
algorithm.

HANNAH: What's that?

VALENTINE: Well, it's . . . Jesus . . . it's an algorithm that's been
. . . iterated. How'm I supposed to . . .? (*He makes an effort.*)
The left-hand pages are graphs of what the numbers are doing
on the right-hand pages. But all on different scales. Each
graph is a small section of the previous one, blown up. Like
you'd blow up a detail of a photograph, and then a detail of the
detail, and so on, forever. Or in her case, till she ran out of pages.

HANNAH: Is it difficult?

VALENTINE: The maths isn't difficult. It's what you did at school. You have some x-and-y equation. Any value for x gives you a value for y. So you put a dot where it's right for both x and y. Then you take the next value for x which gives you another value for y, and when you've done that a few times you join up the dots and that's your graph of whatever the equation is.

HANNAH: And is that what she's doing?

VALENTINE: No. Not exactly. Not at all. What she's doing is, every time she works out a value for y, she's using *that* as her next value for x. And so on. Like a feedback. She's feeding the solution back into the equation, and then solving it again. Iteration, you see.

HANNAH: And that's surprising, is it?

VALENTINE: Well, it is a bit. It's the technique I'm using on my grouse numbers, and it hasn't been around for much longer than, well, call it twenty years.

(*Pause.*)

HANNAH: Why would she be doing it?

VALENTINE: I have no idea.

(*Pause.*)

I thought you were doing the hermit.

HANNAH: I am. I still am. But Bernard, damn him . . . Thomasina's tutor turns out to have interesting connections. Bernard is going through the library like a bloodhound. The portfolio was in a cupboard.

VALENTINE: There's a lot of stuff around. Gus loves going through it. No old masters or anything . . .

HANNAH: The maths primer she was using belonged to him – the tutor; he wrote his name in it.

VALENTINE: (*Reading*) 'Septimus Hodge.'

HANNAH: Why were these things saved, do you think?

VALENTINE: Why should there be a reason?

HANNAH: And the diagram, what's it of?

VALENTINE: How would I know?

HANNAH: Why are you cross?

VALENTINE: I'm not cross. (*Pause.*) When your Thomasina was

44

doing maths it had been the same maths for a couple of thousand years. Classical. And for a century after Thomasina. Then maths left the real world behind, just like modern art, really. Nature was classical, maths was suddenly Picassos. But now nature is having the last laugh. The freaky stuff is turning out to be the mathematics of the natural world.

HANNAH: This feedback thing?

VALENTINE: For example.

HANNAH: Well, could Thomasina have –

VALENTINE: (*Snaps*) No, of course she bloody couldn't!

HANNAH: All right, you're not cross. What did you mean you were doing the same thing she was doing? (*Pause.*) What *are* you doing?

VALENTINE: Actually I'm doing it from the other end. She started with an equation and turned it into a graph. I've got a graph – real data – and I'm trying to find the equation which would give you the graph if you used it the way she's used hers. Iterated it.

HANNAH: What for?

VALENTINE: It's how you look at population changes in biology. Goldfish in a pond, say. This year there are x goldfish. Next year there'll be y goldfish. Some get born, some get eaten by herons, whatever. Nature manipulates the x and turns it into y. Then y goldfish is your starting population for the following year. Just like Thomasina. Your value for y becomes your next value for x. The question is: what is being done to x? What is the manipulation? Whatever it is, it can be written down as mathematics. It's called an algorithm.

HANNAH: It can't be the same every year.

VALENTINE: The details change, you can't keep tabs on everything, it's not nature in a box. But it isn't necessary to know the details. When they are all put together, it turns out the population is obeying a mathematical rule.

HANNAH: The goldfish are?

VALENTINE: Yes. No. The numbers. It's not about the behaviour of fish. It's about the behaviour of numbers. This thing works for any phenomenon which eats its own numbers –

measles epidemics, rainfall averages, cotton prices, it's a natural phenomenon in itself. Spooky.

HANNAH: Does it work for grouse?

VALENTINE: I don't know yet. I mean, it does undoubtedly, but it's hard to show. There's more noise with grouse.

HANNAH: Noise?

VALENTINE: Distortions. Interference. Real data is messy. There's a thousand acres of moorland that had grouse on it, always did till about 1930. But nobody counted the grouse. They shot them. So you count the grouse they shot. But burning the heather interferes, it improves the food supply. A good year for foxes interferes the other way, they eat the chicks. And then there's the weather. It's all very, very noisy out there. Very hard to spot the tune. Like a piano in the next room, it's playing your song, but unfortunately it's out of whack, some of the strings are missing, and the pianist is tone deaf and drunk – I mean, the *noise*! Impossible!

HANNAH: What do you do?

VALENTINE: You start guessing what the tune might be. You try to pick it out of the noise. You try this, you try that, you start to get something – it's half-baked but you start putting in notes which are missing or not quite the right notes . . . and bit by bit . . . (*He starts to dumdi-da to the tune of 'Happy Birthday'.*) Dumdi-dum-dum, dear Val-en-tine, dumdi-dum-dum to you – the lost algorithm!

HANNAH: (*Soberly*) Yes, I see. And then what?

VALENTINE: I publish.

HANNAH: Of course. Sorry. Jolly good.

VALENTINE: That's the theory. Grouse are bastards compared to goldfish.

HANNAH: Why did you choose them?

VALENTINE: The game books. My true inheritance. Two hundred years of real data on a plate.

HANNAH: Somebody wrote down everything that's shot?

VALENTINE: Well, that's what a game book is. I'm only using from 1870, when butts and beaters came in.

HANNAH: You mean the game books go back to Thomasina's time?

VALENTINE: Oh yes. Further. (*And then getting ahead of her thought.*) No – really. I promise you. I *promise* you. Not a schoolgirl living in a country house in Derbyshire in eighteen-something!

HANNAH: Well, what was she doing?

VALENTINE: She was just playing with the numbers. The truth is, she wasn't doing anything.

HANNAH: She must have been doing something.

VALENTINE: Doodling. Nothing she understood.

HANNAH: A monkey at a typewriter?

VALENTINE: Yes. Well, a piano.

(HANNAH *picks up the algebra book and reads from it.*)

HANNAH: '. . . a method whereby all the forms of nature must give up their numerical secrets and draw themselves through number alone.' This feedback, is it a way of making pictures of forms in nature? Just tell me if it is or it isn't.

VALENTINE: (*Irritated*) To *me* it is. Pictures of turbulence – growth – change – creation – it's not a way of drawing an elephant, for God's sake!

HANNAH: I'm sorry.

(*She picks up an apple leaf from the table. She is timid about pushing the point.*)

So you couldn't make a picture of this leaf by iterating a whatsit?

VALENTINE: (*Off-hand*) Oh yes, you could do that.

HANNAH: (*Furiously*) Well, tell me! Honestly, I could kill you!

VALENTINE: If you knew the algorithm and fed it back say ten thousand times, each time there'd be a dot somewhere on the screen. You'd never know where to expect the next dot. But gradually you'd start to see this shape, because every dot will be inside the shape of this leaf. It wouldn't *be* a leaf, it would be a mathematical object. But yes. The unpredictable and the predetermined unfold together to make everything the way it is. It's how nature creates itself, on every scale, the snowflake and the snowstorm. It makes me so happy. To be at the beginning again, knowing almost nothing. People were talking about the end of physics. Relativity and quantum looked as if they were going to clean out the whole problem

between them. A theory of everything. But they only explained the very big and the very small. The universe, the elementary particles. The ordinary-sized stuff which is our lives, the things people write poetry about – clouds – daffodils – waterfalls – and what happens in a cup of coffee when the cream goes in – these things are full of mystery, as mysterious to us as the heavens were to the Greeks. We're better at predicting events at the edge of the galaxy or inside the nucleus of an atom than whether it'll rain on auntie's garden party three Sundays from now. Because the problem turns out to be different. We can't even predict the next drip from a dripping tap when it gets irregular. Each drip sets up the conditions for the next, the smallest variation blows prediction apart, and the weather is unpredictable the same way, will always be unpredictable. When you push the numbers through the computer you can see it on the screen. The future is disorder. A door like this has cracked open five or six times since we got up on our hind legs. It's the best possible time to be alive, when almost everything you thought you knew is wrong.
(*Pause.*)

HANNAH: The weather is fairly predictable in the Sahara.

VALENTINE: The scale is different but the graph goes up and down the same way. Six thousand years in the Sahara looks like six months in Manchester, I bet you.

HANNAH: How much?

VALENTINE: Everything you have to lose.

HANNAH: (*Pause*) No.

VALENTINE: Quite right. That's why there was corn in Egypt.
(*Hiatus. The piano is heard again.*)

HANNAH: What is he playing?

VALENTINE: I don't know. He makes it up.

HANNAH: Chloë called him 'genius'.

VALENTINE: It's what my mother calls him – only *she* means it. Last year some expert had her digging in the wrong place for months to find something or other – the foundations of Capability Brown's boat-house – and Gus put her right first go.

HANNAH: Did he ever speak?

VALENTINE: Oh yes. Until he was five. You've never asked about him. You get high marks here for good breeding.

HANNAH: Yes, I know. I've always been given credit for my unconcern.

(BERNARD *enters in high excitement and triumph.*)

BERNARD: *English Bards and Scotch Reviewers.* A pencilled superscription. Listen and kiss my cycle-clips!

(*He is carrying the book. He reads from it.*)

    'O harbinger of Sleep, who missed the press
    And hoped his drone might thus escape redress!
    The wretched Chater, bard of Eros' Couch,
    For his narcotic let my pencil vouch!'

You see, *you have to turn over every page.*

HANNAH: Is it his handwriting?

BERNARD: Oh, come *on.*

HANNAH: Obviously not.

BERNARD: Christ, what do you want?

HANNAH: Proof.

VALENTINE: Quite right. Who are you talking about?

BERNARD: Proof? *Proof?* You'd have to be there, you silly bitch!

VALENTINE: (*Mildly*) I say, you're speaking of my fiancée.

HANNAH: Especially when I have a present for you. Guess what I found. (*Producing the present for* BERNARD.) Lady Croom writing from London to her husband. Her brother, Captain Brice, married a Mrs Chater. In other words, one might assume, a widow.

(BERNARD *looks at the letter.*)

BERNARD: I *said* he was dead. What year? 1810! Oh my God, 1810! Well *done*, Hannah! Are you going to tell me it's a different Mrs Chater?

HANNAH: Oh no. It's her all right. Note her Christian name.

BERNARD: Charity. Charity . . . 'Deny what cannot be proven for Charity's sake!'

HANNAH: Don't kiss me!

VALENTINE: She won't let anyone kiss her.

BERNARD: You see! They wrote – they scribbled – they put it on paper. It was their employment. Their diversion. Paper is what they had. And there'll be more. There is always more. We can find it!

HANNAH: Such passion. First Valentine, now you. It's moving.

BERNARD: The aristocratic friend of the tutor – under the same roof as the poor sod whose book he savaged – the first thing he does is seduce Chater's wife. All is discovered. There is a duel. Chater dead, Byron fled! P.S. guess what?, the widow married her ladyship's brother! Do you honestly think no one wrote a word? How could they not! It dropped from sight but we will write it again!

HANNAH: You can, Bernard. I'm not going to take any credit, I haven't done anything.

(*The same thought has clearly occurred to* BERNARD. *He becomes instantly po-faced.*)

BERNARD: Well, that's – very fair – generous –

HANNAH: Prudent. Chater could have died of anything, anywhere.

(*The po-face is forgotten.*)

BERNARD: But he fought a duel with Byron!

HANNAH: You haven't established it was fought. You haven't established it was Byron. For God's sake, Bernard, you haven't established Byron was even here!

BERNARD: I'll tell you your problem. No guts.

HANNAH: Really?

BERNARD: By which I mean a visceral belief in yourself. Gut instinct. The part of you which doesn't reason. The certainty for which there is no back-reference. Because time is reversed. Tock, tick goes the universe and then recovers itself, but it was enough, you were in there and you bloody *know*.

VALENTINE: Are you talking about Lord Byron, the poet?

BERNARD: No, you fucking idiot, we're talking about Lord Byron the chartered accountant.

VALENTINE: (*Unoffended*) Oh well, *he* was here all right, the poet.

(*Silence.*)

HANNAH: How do you know?

VALENTINE: He's in the game book. I think he shot a hare. I read through the whole lot once when I had mumps – some quite interesting people –

HANNAH: Where's the book?

VALENTINE: It's not one I'm using – too early, of course –

HANNAH: 1809.

VALENTINE: They've always been in the commode. Ask Chloë.

(HANNAH *looks to* BERNARD. BERNARD *has been silent because he has been incapable of speech. He seems to have gone into a trance, in which only his mouth tries to work.* HANNAH *steps over to him and gives him a demure kiss on the cheek. It works.* BERNARD *lurches out into the garden and can be heard croaking for* 'Chloë . . . Chloë!')

VALENTINE: My mother's lent him her bicycle. Lending one's bicycle is a form of safe sex, possibly the safest there is. My mother is in a flutter about Bernard, and he's no fool. He gave her a first edition of Horace Walpole, and now she's lent him her bicycle.

(*He gathers up the three items [the primer, the lesson book and the diagram] and puts them into the portfolio.*)

Can I keep these for a while?

HANNAH: Yes, of course.

(*The piano stops.* GUS *enters hesitantly from the music room.*)

VALENTINE: (*To* GUS) Yes, finished . . . coming now. (*To* HANNAH) I'm trying to work out the diagram.

(GUS *nods and smiles, at* HANNAH *too, but she is preoccupied.*)

HANNAH: What I don't understand is . . . why nobody did this feedback thing before – it's not like relativity, you don't have to be Einstein.

VALENTINE: You couldn't see to look before. The electronic calculator was what the telescope was for Galileo.

HANNAH: Calculator?

VALENTINE: There wasn't enough time before. There weren't enough *pencils*! (*He flourishes Thomasina's lesson book.*) This took her I don't know how many days and she hasn't scratched the paintwork. Now she'd only have to press a button, the same button over and over. Iteration. A few minutes. And what I've done in a couple of months, with only a *pencil* the calculations would take me the rest of my life to do again – thousands of pages – tens of thousands! And so boring!

HANNAH: Do you mean – ?

(*She stops because* GUS *is plucking* VALENTINE'S *sleeve.*)
Do you mean – ?

VALENTINE: All right, Gus, I'm coming.

HANNAH: Do you mean that was the only problem? Enough time? And paper? And the boredom?

VALENTINE: We're going to get out the dressing-up box.

HANNAH: (*Driven to raising her voice*) Val! Is that what you're saying?

VALENTINE: (*Surprised by her. Mildly*) No, I'm saying you'd have to have a reason for doing it.

(GUS *runs out of the room, upset.*)

(*Apologetically*) He hates people shouting.

HANNAH: I'm sorry.

(VALENTINE *starts to follow* GUS.)

But anything else?

VALENTINE: Well, the other thing is, you'd have to be insane.

(VALENTINE *leaves.*

HANNAH *stays, thoughtful. After a moment, she turns to the table and picks up the* Cornhill Magazine. *She looks into it briefly, then closes it, and leaves the room, taking the magazine with her.*

The empty room.

The light changes to early morning. From a long way off, there is a pistol shot. A moment later there is the cry of dozens of crows disturbed from the unseen trees.)

ACT TWO

SCENE FIVE

BERNARD *is pacing around, reading aloud from a handful of typed sheets.* VALENTINE, CHLOË *and* GUS *are his audience.* GUS *sits somewhat apart, perhaps less attentive.* VALENTINE *has his tortoise and is eating a sandwich from which he extracts shreds of lettuce to offer the tortoise.*

BERNARD: 'Did it happen? Could it happen?

Undoubtedly it could. Only three years earlier the Irish poet Tom Moore appeared on the field of combat to avenge a review by Jeffrey of the *Edinburgh*. These affairs were seldom fatal and sometimes farcical but, potentially, the duellist stood in respect to the law no differently from a murderer. As for the murderee, a minor poet like Ezra Chater could go to his death in a Derbyshire glade as unmissed and unremembered as his contemporary and namesake, the minor botanist who died in the forests of the West Indies, lost to history like the monkey that bit him. On April 16th 1809, a few days after he left Sidley Park, Byron wrote to his solicitor John Hanson: 'If the consequences of my leaving England were ten times as ruinous as you describe, I have no alternative; there are circumstances which render it absolutely indispensable, and quit the country I must immediately.' To which, the editor's note in the Collected Letters reads as follows: 'What Byron's urgent reasons for leaving England were at this time has never been revealed.' The letter was written from the family seat, Newstead Abbey, Nottinghamshire. A long day's ride to the north-west lay Sidley Park, the estate of the Coverlys – a far grander family, raised by Charles II to the Earldom of Croom . . .'

(HANNAH *enters briskly, a piece of paper in her hand.*)

HANNAH: Bernard . . .! Val . . .

BERNARD: Do you mind?

(HANNAH *puts her piece of paper down in front of* VALENTINE.)

CHLOË: (*Angrily*) *Hannah!*

HANNAH: What?

53

CHLOË: She's so *rude*!

HANNAH: (*Taken aback*) What? Am I?

VALENTINE: Bernard's reading us his lecture.

HANNAH: Yes, I know. (*Then recollecting herself.*) Yes – yes – that *was* rude. I'm sorry, Bernard.

VALENTINE: (*With the piece of paper*) What is this?

HANNAH: (To BERNARD) Spot on – the India Office Library. (*To* VALENTINE) Peacock's letter in holograph, I got a copy sent –

CHLOË: *Hannah!* Shut up!

HANNAH: (*Sitting down*) Yes, sorry.

BERNARD: It's all right, I'll read it to myself.

CHLOË: *No.*

(HANNAH *reaches for the Peacock letter and takes it back.*)

HANNAH: Go on, Bernard. Have I missed anything? Sorry.

(BERNARD *stares at her balefully but then continues to read.*)

BERNARD: 'The Byrons of Newstead in 1809 comprised an eccentric widow and her undistinguished son, the "lame brat", who until the age of ten when he came into the title, had been carted about the country from lodging to lodging by his vulgar hectoring monster of a mother – ' (HANNAH's *hand has gone up*) – overruled – 'and who four months past his twenty-first birthday was master of nothing but his debts and his genius. Between the Byrons and the Coverlys there was no social equality and none to be expected. The connection, undisclosed to posterity until now, was with Septimus Hodge, Byron's friend at Harrow and Trinity College – ' (HANNAH's *hand goes up again*) – sustained – (*He makes an instant correction with a silver pencil.*) 'Byron's contemporary at Harrow and Trinity College, and now tutor in residence to the Croom daughter, Thomasina Coverly. Byron's letters tell us where he was on April 8th and on April 12th. He was at Newstead. But on the 10th he was at Sidley Park, as attested by the game book preserved there: "April 10th 1809 – forenoon. High cloud, dry, and sun between times, wind southeasterly. Self – Augustus – Lord Byron. Fourteen pigeon, one hare (Lord B.)." But, as we know now, the drama of life and death at Sidley Park was not about pigeons but about sex and literature.'

VALENTINE: Unless you were the pigeon.

BERNARD: I don't have to do this. I'm paying you a compliment.

CHLOË: Ignore him, Bernard – go on, get to the duel.

BERNARD: Hannah's not even paying attention.

HANNAH: Yes I am, it's all going in. I often work with the radio
on.

BERNARD: Oh thanks!

HANNAH: Is there much more?

CHLOË: *Hannah!*

HANNAH: No, it's fascinating. I just wondered how much more
there was. I need to ask Valentine about this (*letter*) – sorry,
Bernard, go on, this will keep.

VALENTINE: Yes – sorry, Bernard.

CHLOË: Please, Bernard!

BERNARD: Where was I?

VALENTINE: Pigeons.

CHLOË: Sex.

HANNAH: Literature.

BERNARD: Life and death. Right. 'Nothing could be more
eloquent of that than the three documents I have quoted: the
terse demand to settle a matter in private; the desperate
scribble of "my husband has sent for pistols"; and on April
11th, the gauntlet thrown down by the aggrieved and
cuckolded author Ezra Chater. The covers have not
survived. What is certain is that all three letters were in
Byron's possession when his books were sold in 1816 –
preserved in the pages of "The Couch of Eros" which seven
years earlier at Sidley Park Byron had borrowed from
Septimus Hodge.'

HANNAH: Borrowed?

BERNARD: I will be taking questions at the end. Constructive
comments will be welcome. Which is indeed my reason for
trying out in the provinces before my London opening under
the auspices of the Byron Society prior to publication. By the
way, Valentine, do you want a credit? – 'the game book
recently discovered by.'?

VALENTINE: It was never lost, Bernard.

BERNARD: 'As recently pointed out by.' I don't normally like giving credit where it's due, but with scholarly articles as with divorce, there is a certain cachet in citing a member of the aristocracy. I'll pop it in ad lib for the lecture, and give you a mention in the press release. How's that?

VALENTINE: Very kind.

HANNAH: Press release? What happened to the *Journal of English Studies*?

BERNARD: That comes later with the apparatus, and in the recognized tone – very dry, very modest, absolutely gloat-free, and yet unmistakably 'Eat your heart out, you dozy bastards'. But first, it's 'Media Don, book early to avoid disappointment'. Where was I?

VALENTINE: Game book.

CHLOË: Eros.

HANNAH: Borrowed.

BERNARD: Right. ' – borrowed from Septimus Hodge. Is it conceivable that the letters were already in the book when Byron borrowed it?'

VALENTINE: Yes.

CHLOË: Shut up, Val.

VALENTINE: Well, it's conceivable.

BERNARD: 'Is it *likely* that Hodge would have lent Byron the book without first removing the three private letters?'

VALENTINE: Look, sorry – I only meant, Byron could have borrowed the book without asking.

HANNAH: That's true.

BERNARD: Then why wouldn't Hodge get them back?

HANNAH: I don't know, I wasn't there.

BERNARD: That's right, you bloody weren't.

CHLOË: Go on, Bernard.

BERNARD: 'It is the third document, the challenge itself, that convinces. Chater "as a man and a poet", points the finger at his "slanderer in the press". Neither as a man nor a poet did Ezra Chater cut such a figure as to be habitually slandered or even mentioned in the press. It is surely indisputable that the slander was the review of "The Maid of Turkey" in the *Piccadilly Recreation*. Did Septimus Hodge have any connection with the London periodicals? No. Did Byron?

56

Yes! He had reviewed Wordsworth two years earlier, he was to review Spencer two years later. And do we have any clue as to Byron's opinion of Chater the poet? Yes! Who but Byron could have written the four lines pencilled into Lady Croom's copy of *English Bards and Scotch Reviewers'* –

HANNAH: Almost anybody.

BERNARD: Darling –

HANNAH: Don't call me darling.

BERNARD: Dickhead, then, is it likely that the man Chater calls his friend Septimus Hodge is the same man who screwed his wife and kicked the shit out of his last book?

HANNAH: Put it like that, almost certain.

CHLOË: (*Earnestly*) You've been deeply wounded in the past, haven't you, Hannah?

HANNAH: Nothing compared to listening to this. Why is there nothing in Byron's letters about the *Piccadilly* reviews?

BERNARD: Exactly. Because he killed the author.

HANNAH: But the first one, 'The Maid of Turkey', was the year before. Was he clairvoyant?

CHLOË: Letters get lost.

BERNARD: Thank you! Exactly! There is a platonic letter which confirms everything – lost but ineradicable, like radio voices rippling through the universe for all eternity. 'My dear Hodge – here I am in Albania and you're the only person in the whole world who knows why. Poor C! I never wished him any harm – except in the *Piccadilly*, of course – it was the woman who bade me eat, dear Hodge! – what a tragic business, but thank God it ended well for poetry. Yours ever, B. – PS. Burn this.'

VALENTINE: How did Chater find out the reviewer was Byron?

BERNARD: (*Irritated*) I don't know, I wasn't there, was I? (*Pause. To* HANNAH) You wish to say something?

HANNAH: Moi?

CHLOË: I know. Byron told Mrs Chater in bed. Next day he dumped her so she grassed on him, and pleaded date rape.

BERNARD: (*Fastidiously*) Date rape? What do you mean, date rape?

HANNAH: April the tenth.

57

(BERNARD *cracks. Everything becomes loud and overlapped as* BERNARD *threatens to walk out and is cajoled into continuing*.)

BERNARD: Right! – forget it!

HANNAH: Sorry –

BERNARD: No – I've had nothing but sarcasm and childish interruptions –

VALENTINE: What did I do?

BERNARD: No credit for probably the most sensational literary discovery of the century –

CHLOË: I think you're jolly unfair – they're jealous, Bernard –

HANNAH: I won't say another word –

VALENTINE: Yes, go on, Bernard – we promise.

BERNARD: (*Finally*) Well, only if you stop *feeding tortoises*!

VALENTINE: Well, it's his lunch time.

BERNARD: And on condition that I am afforded the common courtesy of a scholar among scholars –

HANNAH: Absolutely mum till you're finished –

BERNARD: After which, any comments are to be couched in terms of accepted academic –

HANNAH: Dignity – you're right, Bernard.

BERNARD: – respect.

HANNAH: Respect. Absolutely. The language of scholars. Count on it.

(*Having made a great show of putting his pages away,* BERNARD *reassembles them and finds his place, glancing suspiciously at the other three for signs of levity*.)

BERNARD: Last paragraph. 'Without question, Ezra Chater issued a challenge to *somebody*. If a duel was fought in the dawn mist of Sidley Park in April 1809, his opponent, on the evidence, was a critic with a gift for ridicule and a taste for seduction. Do we need to look far? Without question, Mrs Chater was a widow by 1810. If we seek the occasion of Ezra Chater's early and unrecorded death, do we need to look far? Without question, Lord Byron, in the very season of his emergence as a literary figure, quit the country in a cloud of panic and mystery, and stayed abroad for two years at a time when Continental travel was unusual and dangerous. If we seek his reason – *do we need to look far?*

*(No mean performer, he is pleased with the effect of his
peroration. There is a significant silence.)*

HANNAH: Bollocks.

CHLOË: Well, I think it's true.

HANNAH: You've left out everything which doesn't fit. Byron had
  been banging on for months about leaving England – there's
  a letter in *February* –

BERNARD: But he didn't go, did he?

HANNAH: And then he didn't sail until the beginning of July!

BERNARD: Everything moved more slowly then. Time was
  different. He was two weeks in Falmouth waiting for wind or
  something –

HANNAH: Bernard, I don't know why I'm bothering – you're
  arrogant, greedy and reckless. You've gone from a glint in
  your eye to a sure thing in a hop, skip and a jump. You
  deserve what you get and I think you're mad. But I can't
  help myself, you're like some exasperating child pedalling its
  tricycle towards the edge of a cliff, and I have to do
  something. So listen to me. If Byron killed Chater in a duel
  I'm Marie of Romania. You'll end up with so much *fame* you
  won't leave the house without a paper bag over your head.

VALENTINE: Actually, Bernard, as a scientist, your theory is
  incomplete.

BERNARD: But I'm not a scientist.

VALENTINE: *(Patiently)* No, *as a scientist* –

BERNARD: *(Beginning to shout)* I have yet to hear a proper
  argument.

HANNAH: Nobody would kill a man and then pan his book. I
  mean, not in that order. So he must have borrowed the book,
  written the review, *posted it*, seduced Mrs Chater, fought a
  duel and departed, all in the space of two or three days. Who
  would do that?

BERNARD: Byron.

HANNAH: It's hopeless.

BERNARD: You've never understood him, as you've shown in
  your novelette.

HANNAH: In my what?

BERNARD: Oh, sorry – did you think it was a work of historical

revisionism? Byron the spoilt child promoted beyond his
gifts by the spirit of the age! And Caroline the closet
intellectual shafted by a male society!

VALENTINE: I read that somewhere –

HANNAH: It's his review.

BERNARD: And bloody well said, too!

(*Things are turning a little ugly and* BERNARD *seems in a mood
to push them that way.*)

You got them backwards, darling. Caroline was Romantic
waffle on wheels with no talent, and Byron was an
eighteenth-century Rationalist touched by genius. And he
killed Chater.

HANNAH: (*Pause*) If it's not too late to change my mind, I'd like
you to go ahead.

BERNARD: I intend to. Look to the mote in your own eye! – you
even had the wrong bloke on the dust-jacket!

HANNAH: Dust-jacket?

VALENTINE: What about my computer model? Aren't you going
to mention it?

BERNARD: It's inconclusive.

VALENTINE: (*To* HANNAH) The *Piccadilly* reviews aren't a very
good fit with Byron's other reviews, you see.

HANNAH: (*To* BERNARD) What do you mean, the wrong bloke?

BERNARD: (*Ignoring her*) The other reviews aren't a very good fit
for each other, are they?

VALENTINE: No, but differently. The parameters –

BERNARD: (*Jeering*) Parameters! You can't stick Byron's head in
your laptop! Genius isn't like your average grouse.

VALENTINE: (*Casually*) Well, it's all trivial anyway.

BERNARD: What is?

VALENTINE: Who wrote what when . . .

BERNARD: Trivial?

VALENTINE: Personalities.

BERNARD: I'm sorry – did you say trivial?

VALENTINE: It's a technical term.

BERNARD: Not where I come from, it isn't.

VALENTINE: The questions you're asking don't matter, you see.
It's like arguing who got there first with the calculus. The

English say Newton, the Germans say Leibnitz. But it doesn't *matter*. Personalities. What matters is the calculus. Scientific progress. Knowledge.

BERNARD: Really? Why?

VALENTINE: Why what?

BERNARD: Why does scientific progress matter more than personalities?

VALENTINE: Is he serious?

HANNAH: No, he's trivial. Bernard –

VALENTINE: (*Interrupting, to* BERNARD) Do yourself a favour, you're on a loser.

BERNARD: Oh, you're going to zap me with penicillin and pesticides. Spare me that and I'll spare you the bomb and aerosols. But don't confuse progress with perfectibility. A great poet is always timely. A great philosopher is an urgent need. There's no rush for Isaac Newton. We were quite happy with Aristotle's cosmos. Personally, I preferred it. Fifty-five crystal spheres geared to God's crankshaft is my idea of a satisfying universe. I can't think of anything more trivial than the speed of light. Quarks, quasars – big bangs, black holes – who gives a shit? How did you people con us out of all that status? All that money? And why are you so pleased with yourselves?

CHLOË: Are you against penicillin, Bernard?

BERNARD: Don't feed the animals. (*Back to* VALENTINE) I'd push the lot of you over a cliff myself. Except the one in the wheelchair, I think I'd lose the sympathy vote before people had time to think it through.

HANNAH: (*Loudly*) What the hell do you mean, the dust-jacket?

BERNARD: (*Ignoring her*) If knowledge isn't self-knowledge it isn't doing much, mate. Is the universe expanding? Is it contracting? Is it standing on one leg and singing 'When Father Painted the Parlour'? Leave me out. I can expand my universe without you. 'She walks in beauty, like the night of cloudless climes and starry skies, and all that's best of dark and bright meet in her aspect and her eyes.' There you are, he wrote it after coming home from a party. (*With offensive politeness.*) What is it that you're doing with grouse, Valentine, I'd love to know?

(VALENTINE *stands up and it is suddenly apparent that he is shaking and close to tears.*)

VALENTINE: (*To* CHLOË) He's not against penicillin, and he knows I'm not against poetry. (*To* BERNARD) I've given up on the grouse.

HANNAH: You haven't, Valentine!

VALENTINE: (*Leaving*) I can't do it.

HANNAH: *Why?*

VALENTINE: Too much noise. There's just too much *bloody noise!* (*On which,* VALENTINE *leaves the room.* CHLOË, *upset and in tears, jumps up and briefly pummels* BERNARD *ineffectually with her fists.*)

CHLOË: You bastard, Bernard!

(*She follows* VALENTINE *out and is followed at a run by* GUS. *Pause.*)

HANNAH: Well, I think that's everybody. You can leave now, give Lightning a kick on your way out.

BERNARD: Yes, I'm sorry about that. It's no fun when it's not among pros, is it?

HANNAH: No.

BERNARD: Oh, well . . . (*he begins to put his lecture sheets away in his briefcase, and is thus reminded . . .*) do you want to know about your book jacket? 'Lord Byron and Caroline Lamb at the Royal Academy'? Ink study by Henry Fuseli?

HANNAH: What about it?

BERNARD: It's not them.

HANNAH: (*She explodes*) Who says!?

(BERNARD *brings the* Byron Society Journal *from his briefcase.*)

BERNARD: This Fuseli expert in the *Byron Society Journal.* They sent me the latest . . . as a distinguished guest speaker.

HANNAH: But of course it's them! Everyone knows –

BERNARD: Popular tradition only. (*He is finding the place in the journal.*) Here we are. 'No earlier than 1820'. He's analysed it. (*Offers it to her.*) Read at your leisure.

HANNAH: (*She sounds like* BERNARD *jeering*) Analysed it?

BERNARD: Charming sketch, of course, but Byron was in Italy . . .

HANNAH: But, Bernard – I *know* it's them.

BERNARD: How?

HANNAH: How? It just *is*. 'Analysed it', my big toe!

BERNARD: Language!

HANNAH: He's wrong.

BERNARD: Oh, gut instinct, you mean?

HANNAH: (*Flatly*) He's wrong.

(BERNARD *snaps shut his briefcase*.)

BERNARD: Well, it's all trivial, isn't it? Why don't you come?

HANNAH: Where?

BERNARD: With me.

HANNAH: To London? What for?

BERNARD: What for.

HANNAH: Oh, your lecture.

BERNARD: No, no, bugger that. Sex.

HANNAH: Oh . . . No. Thanks . . . (*then, protesting*) *Bernard*!

BERNARD: You should try it. It's very underrated.

HANNAH: Nothing against it.

BERNARD: Yes, you have. You should let yourself go a bit. You might have written a better book. Or at any rate the right book.

HANNAH: Sex and literature. Literature and sex. Your conversation, left to itself, doesn't have many places to go. Like two marbles rolling around a pudding basin. One of them is always sex.

BERNARD: Ah well, yes. Men all over.

HANNAH: No doubt. Einstein – relativity and sex. Chippendale – sex and furniture. Galileo – 'Did the earth move?' What the hell is it with you people? Chaps sometimes wanted to marry me, and I don't know a worse bargain. Available sex against not being allowed to fart in bed. What do you mean the right book?

BERNARD: It takes a romantic to make a heroine of Caroline Lamb. You were cut out for Byron.

(*Pause*.)

HANNAH: So, cheerio.

BERNARD: Oh, I'm coming back for the dance, you know. Chloë asked me.

HANNAH: She meant well, but I don't dance.

BERNARD: No, no – I'm going with her.

HANNAH: Oh, I see. I don't, actually.

BERNARD: I'm her date. Sub rosa. Don't tell Mother.

HANNAH: She doesn't want her mother to know?

BERNARD: No – *I* don't want her mother to know. This is my first experience of the landed aristocracy. I tell you, I'm boggle-eyed.

HANNAH: Bernard! – you haven't seduced that girl?

BERNARD: Seduced her? Every time I turned round she was up a library ladder. In the end I gave in. That reminds me – I spotted something between her legs that made me think of you. (*He instantly receives a sharp stinging slap on the face but manages to remain completely unperturbed by it. He is already producing from his pocket a small book. His voice has hardly hesitated.*)

The Peaks Traveller and Gazetteer – James Godolphin 1832 – unillustrated, I'm afraid. (*He has opened the book to a marked place.*) Sidley Park in Derbyshire, property of the Earl of Croom . . .'

HANNAH: (*Numbly*) The world is going to hell in a handcart.

BERNARD: 'Five hundred acres including forty of lake – the Park by Brown and Noakes has pleasing features in the horrid style – viaduct, grotto, etc – a hermitage occupied by a lunatic since twenty years without discourse or companion save for a pet tortoise, Plautus by name, which he suffers children to touch on request.' (*He holds out the book for her.*) A tortoise. They must be a feature.

(*After a moment* HANNAH *takes the book.*)

HANNAH: Thank you.

(VALENTINE *comes to the door.*)

VALENTINE: The station taxi is at the front . . .

BERNARD: Yes . . . thanks . . . Oh – did Peacock come up trumps?

HANNAH: For some.

BERNARD: Hermit's name and CV?

(*He picks up and glances at the Peacock letter.*)

'My dear Thackeray . . .' God, I'm good.

(*He puts the letter down.*)

Well, wish me luck – (*Vaguely to* VALENTINE) Sorry about
. . . you know . . . (*and to* HANNAH) and about your . . .

VALENTINE: Piss off, Bernard.

BERNARD: Right.

(BERNARD *goes.*)

HANNAH: Don't let Bernard get to you. It's only performance art,
you know. Rhetoric. they used to teach it in ancient times,
like PT. It's not about being right, they had philosophy for
that. Rhetoric was their chat show. Bernard's indignation is a
sort of aerobics for when he gets on television.

VALENTINE: I don't care to be rubbished by the dustbin man.
(*He has been looking at the letter.*) The what of the lunatic?
(HANNAH *reclaims the letter and reads it for him.*)

HANNAH: 'The testament of the lunatic serves as a caution against
French fashion . . . for it was Frenchified mathematick that
brought him to the melancholy certitude of a world without
light or life . . . as a wooden stove that must consume itself
until ash and stove are as one, and heat is gone from the
earth.'

VALENTINE: (*Amused, surprised*) Huh!

HANNAH: 'He died aged two score years and seven, hoary as Job
and meagre as a cabbage-stalk, the proof of his prediction
even yet unyielding to his labours for the restitution of hope
through good English algebra.'

VALENTINE: That's it?

HANNAH: (*Nods*) Is there anything in it?

VALENTINE: In what? We are all doomed? (*Casually.*) Oh yes,
sure – it's called the second law of thermodynamics.

HANNAH: Was it known about?

VALENTINE: By poets and lunatics from time immemorial.

HANNAH: Seriously.

VALENTINE: No.

HANNAH: Is it anything to do with . . . you know, Thomasina's
discovery?

VALENTINE: She didn't discover anything.

HANNAH: Her lesson book.

VALENTINE: No.

HANNAH: A coincidence, then?

VALENTINE: What is?

HANNAH: (*Reading*) 'He died aged two score years and seven.'
That was in 1834. So he was born in 1787. So was the tutor.
He says so in his letter to Lord Croom when he
recommended himself for the job: 'Date of birth – 1787.'
The hermit was born in the same year as Septimus Hodge.

VALENTINE: (*Pause*) Did Bernard bite you in the leg?

HANNAH: Don't you see? I thought my hermit was a perfect
symbol. An idiot in the landscape. But this is better. The
Age of Enlightenment banished into the Romantic
wilderness! The genius of Sidley Park living on in a hermit's
hut!

VALENTINE: You don't *know* that.

HANNAH: Oh, but I do. I do. Somewhere there will be *something*
. . . if only I can find it.

The room is empty.

A reprise: early morning – a distant pistol shot – the sound of the crows.

JELLABY *enters the dawn-dark room with a lamp. He goes to the windows and looks out. He sees something. He returns to put the lamp on the table, and then opens one of the french windows and steps outside.*

JELLABY: (*Outside*) Mr Hodge!

(SEPTIMUS *comes in, followed by* JELLABY, *who closes the garden door.* SEPTIMUS *is wearing a greatcoat.*)

SEPTIMUS: Thank you, Jellaby. I was expecting to be locked out. What time is it?

JELLABY: Half past five.

SEPTIMUS: That is what I have. Well! – what a bracing experience!

(*He produces two pistols from inside his coat and places them on the table.*)

The dawn, you know. Unexpectedly lively. Fishes, birds, frogs . . . rabbits . . . (*he produces a dead rabbit from inside his coat*) and very beautiful. If only it did not occur so early in the day. I have brought Lady Thomasina a rabbit. Will you take it?

JELLABY: It's dead.

SEPTIMUS: Yes. Lady Thomasina loves a rabbit pie.

(JELLABY *takes the rabbit without enthusiasm. There is a little blood on it.*)

JELLABY: You were missed, Mr Hodge.

SEPTIMUS: I decided to sleep last night in the boat-house. Did I see a carriage leaving the Park?

JELLABY: Captain Brice's carriage, with Mr and Mrs Chater also.

SEPTIMUS: Gone?!

JELLABY: Yes, sir. And Lord Byron's horse was brought round at four o'clock.

SEPTIMUS: Lord Byron too!

JELLABY: Yes, sir. The house has been up and hopping.

SEPTIMUS: But I have his rabbit pistols! What am I to do with his rabbit pistols?

JELLABY: You were looked for in your room.

SEPTIMUS: By whom?

JELLABY: By her ladyship.

SEPTIMUS: In my room?

JELLABY: I will tell her ladyship you are returned.

(*He starts to leave.*)

SEPTIMUS: Jellaby! Did Lord Byron leave a book for me?

JELLABY: A book?

SEPTIMUS: He had the loan of a book from me.

JELLABY: His lordship left nothing in his room, sir, not a coin.

SEPTIMUS: Oh. Well, I'm sure he would have left a coin if he'd had one. Jellaby – here is a half-guinea for you.

JELLABY: Thank you very much, sir.

SEPTIMUS: What has occurred?

JELLABY: The servants are told nothing, sir.

SEPTIMUS: Come, come, does a half-guinea buy nothing any more?

JELLABY: (*Sighs*) Her ladyship encountered Mrs Chater during the night.

SEPTIMUS: Where?

JELLABY: On the threshold of Lord Byron's room.

SEPTIMUS: Ah. Which one was leaving and which entering?

JELLABY: Mrs Chater was leaving Lord Byron's room.

SEPTIMUS: And where was Mr Chater?

JELLABY: Mr Chater and Captain Brice were drinking cherry brandy. They had the footman to keep the fire up until three o'clock. There was a loud altercation upstairs, and –

(LADY CROOM *enters the room.*)

LADY CROOM: Well, Mr Hodge.

SEPTIMUS: My lady.

LADY CROOM: All this to shoot a hare?

SEPTIMUS: A rabbit. (*She gives him one of her looks.*) No, indeed, a hare, though very rabbit-like –

(JELLABY *is about to leave.*)

LADY CROOM: My infusion.

JELLABY: Yes, my lady.

(*He leaves.* LADY CROOM *is carrying two letters. We have not seen them before. Each has an envelope which has been opened. She flings them on the table.*)

LADY CROOM: How dare you!

SEPTIMUS: I cannot be called to account for what was written in private and read without regard to propriety.

LADY CROOM: Addressed to me!

SEPTIMUS: Left in my room, in the event of my death –

LADY CROOM: Pah! – what earthly use is a love letter from beyond the grave?

SEPTIMUS: As much, surely, as from this side of it. The second letter, however, was not addressed to your ladyship.

LADY CROOM: I have a mother's right to open a letter addressed by you to my daughter, whether in the event of your life, your death, or your imbecility. What do you mean by writing to her of rice pudding when she has just suffered the shock of violent death in our midst?

SEPTIMUS: Whose death?

LADY CROOM: Yours, you wretch!

SEPTIMUS: Yes, I see.

LADY CROOM: I do not know which is the madder of your ravings. One envelope full of rice pudding, the other of the most insolent familiarities regarding several parts of my body, but have no doubt which is the more intolerable to me.

SEPTIMUS: Which?

LADY CROOM: Oh, aren't we saucy when our bags are packed! Your friend has gone before you, and I have despatched the harlot Chater and her husband – and also my brother for bringing them here. Such is the sentence, you see, for choosing unwisely in your acquaintance. Banishment. Lord Byron is a rake and a hypocrite, and the sooner he sails for the Levant the sooner he will find society congenial to his character.

SEPTIMUS: It has been a night of reckoning.

LADY CROOM: Indeed I wish it had passed uneventfully with you and Mr Chater shooting each other with the decorum due to a civilized house. You have no secrets left, Mr Hodge. They

spilled out between shrieks and oaths and tears. It is
fortunate that a lifetime's devotion to the sporting gun has
halved my husband's hearing to the ear he sleeps on.

SEPTIMUS: I'm afraid I have no knowledge of what has occurred.

LADY CROOM: Your trollop was discovered in Lord Byron's
room.

SEPTIMUS: Ah. Discovered by Mr Chater?

LADY CROOM: Who else?

SEPTIMUS: I am very sorry, madam, for having used your
kindness to bring my unworthy friend to your notice. He will
have to give an account of himself to me, you may be sure.
(*Before* LADY CROOM *can respond to this threat,* JELLABY
*enters the room with her 'infusion'. This is quite an elaborate
affair: a pewter tray on small feet on which there is a kettle
suspended over a spirit lamp. There is a cup and saucer and the
silver 'basket' containing the dry leaves for the tea.* JELLABY
*places the tray on the table and is about to offer further assistance
with it.*)

LADY CROOM: I will do it.

JELLABY: Yes, my lady. (*To* SEPTIMUS) Lord Byron left a letter
for you with the valet, sir.

SEPTIMUS: Thank you.
(SEPTIMUS *takes the letter off the tray.* JELLABY *prepares to
leave.* LADY CROOM *eyes the letter.*)

LADY CROOM: When did he do so?

JELLABY: As he was leaving, your ladyship.
(JELLABY *leaves.* SEPTIMUS *puts the letter into his pocket.*)

SEPTIMUS: Allow me.
(*Since she does not object, he pours a cup of tea for her. She
accepts it.*)

LADY CROOM: I do not know if it is proper for you to receive a
letter written in my house from someone not welcome in it.

SEPTIMUS: Very improper, I agree. Lord Byron's want of
delicacy is a grief to his friends, among whom I no longer
count myself. I will not read his letter until I have followed
him through the gates.
(*She considers that for a moment.*)

LADY CROOM: That may excuse the reading but not the writing.

SEPTIMUS: Your ladyship should have lived in the Athens of Pericles! The philosophers would have fought the sculptors for your idle hour!

LADY CROOM: (*Protesting*) Oh, really! . . . (*Protesting less.*) Oh really . . .

(SEPTIMUS *has taken Byron's letter from his pocket and is now setting fire to a corner of it using the little flame from the spirit lamp.*)

Oh . . . really . . .

(*The paper blazes in* SEPTIMUS's *hand and he drops it and lets it burn out on the metal tray.*)

SEPTIMUS: Now there's a thing – a letter from Lord Byron never to be read by a living soul. I will take my leave, madam, at the time of your desiring it.

LADY CROOM: To the Indies?

SEPTIMUS: The Indies! Why?

LADY CROOM: To follow the Chater, of course. She did not tell you?

SEPTIMUS: She did not exchange half-a-dozen words with me.

LADY CROOM: I expect she did not like to waste the time. The Chater sails with Captain Brice.

SEPTIMUS: Ah. As a member of the crew?

LADY CROOM: No, as wife to Mr Chater, plant-gatherer to my brother's expedition.

SEPTIMUS: I knew he was no poet. I did not know it was botany under the false colours.

LADY CROOM: He is no more a botanist. My brother paid fifty pounds to have him published, and he will pay a hundred and fifty to have Mr Chater picking flowers in the Indies for a year while the wife plays mistress of the Captain's quarters. Captain Brice has fixed his passion on Mrs Chater, and to take her on voyage he has not scrupled to deceive the Admiralty, the Linnean Society and Sir Joseph Banks, botanist to His Majesty at Kew.

SEPTIMUS: Her passion is not as fixed as his.

LADY CROOM: It is a defect of God's humour that he directs our hearts everywhere but to those who have a right to them.

SEPTIMUS: Indeed, madam. (*Pause.*) But is Mr Chater deceived?

71

LADY CROOM: He insists on it, and finds the proof of his wife's virtue in his eagerness to defend it. Captain Brice is *not* deceived but cannot help himself. He would die for her.

SEPTIMUS: I think, my lady, he would have Mr Chater die for her.

LADY CROOM: Indeed, I never knew a woman worth the duel, or the other way about. Your letter to me goes very ill with your conduct to Mrs Chater, Mr Hodge. I have had experience of being betrayed before the ink is dry, but to be betrayed before the pen is even dipped, and with the village noticeboard, what am I to think of such a performance?

SEPTIMUS: My lady, I was alone with my thoughts in the gazebo, when Mrs Chater ran me to ground, and I being in such a passion, in an agony of unrelieved desire –

LADY CROOM: Oh . . . !

SEPTIMUS: – I thought in my madness that the Chater with her skirts over her head would give me the momentary illusion of the happiness to which I dared not put a face.
(*Pause.*)

LADY CROOM: I do not know when I have received a more unusual compliment, Mr Hodge. I hope I am more than a match for Mrs Chater with her head in a bucket. Does she wear drawers?

SEPTIMUS: She does.

LADY CROOM: Yes, I have heard that drawers are being worn now. It is unnatural for women to be got up like jockeys. I cannot approve.
(*She turns with a whirl of skirts and moves to leave.*)
I know nothing of Pericles or the Athenian philosophers. I can spare them an hour, in my sitting room when I have bathed. Seven o'clock. Bring a book.
(*She goes out.* SEPTIMUS *picks up the two letters, the ones he wrote, and starts to burn them in the flame of the spirit lamp.*)

VALENTINE *and* CHLOË *are at the table.* GUS *is in the room.*

CHLOË *is reading from two Saturday newspapers. She is wearing workaday period clothes, a Regency dress, no hat.*

VALENTINE *is pecking at a portable computer. He is wearing unkempt Regency clothes, too.*

The clothes have evidently come from a large wicker laundry hamper, from which GUS *is producing more clothes to try on himself. He finds a Regency coat and starts putting it on.*

The objects on the table now include two geometrical solids, pyramid and cone, about twenty inches high, of the type used in a drawing lesson; and a pot of dwarf dahlias (which do not look like modern dahlias).

CHLOË: 'Even in Arcadia – Sex, Literature and Death at Sidley Park'. Picture of Byron.

VALENTINE: Not of Bernard?

CHLOË: 'Byron Fought Fatal Duel, Says Don' . . . Valentine, do you think I'm the first person to think of this?

VALENTINE: No.

CHLOË: I haven't said yet. The future is all programmed like a computer – that's a proper theory, isn't it?

VALENTINE: The deterministic universe, yes.

CHLOË: Right. Because everything including us is just a lot of atoms bouncing off each other like billiard balls.

VALENTINE: Yes. There was someone, forget his name, 1820s, who pointed out that from Newton's laws you could predict everything to come – I mean, you'd need a computer as big as the universe but the formula would exist.

CHLOË: But it doesn't work, does it?

VALENTINE: No. It turns out the maths is different.

CHLOË: No, it's all because of sex.

VALENTINE: Really?

CHLOË: That's what I think. The universe is deterministic all right, just like Newton said, I mean it's trying to be, but the only thing going wrong is people fancying people who aren't supposed to be in that part of the plan.

VALENTINE: Ah. The attraction that Newton left out. All the way back to the apple in the garden. Yes. (*Pause.*) Yes, I think you're the first person to think of this.

(HANNAH *enters, carrying a tabloid paper, and a mug of tea.*)

HANNAH: Have you seen this? 'Bonking Byron Shot Poet'.

CHLOË: (*Pleased*) Let's see.

(HANNAH *gives her the paper, smiles at* GUS.)

VALENTINE: He's done awfully well, hasn't he? How did they all know?

HANNAH: Don't be ridiculous. (*To* CHLOË) Your father wants it back.

CHLOË: All right.

HANNAH: What a fool.

CHLOË: Jealous. I think it's brilliant. (*She gets up to go. To* GUS) Yes, that's perfect, but not with trainers. Come on, I'll lend you a pair of flatties, they'll look period on you –

HANNAH: Hello, Gus. You all look so romantic.

(GUS *following* CHLOË *out, hesitates, smiles at her.*)

CHLOË: (*Pointedly*) Are you coming?

(*She holds the door for* GUS *and follows him out, leaving a sense of her disapproval behind her.*)

HANNAH: The important thing is not to give two monkeys for what young people think about you.

(*She goes to look at the other newspapers.*)

VALENTINE: (*Anxiously*) You don't think she's getting a thing about Bernard, do you?

HANNAH: I wouldn't worry about Chloë, she's old enough to vote on her back. 'Byron Fought Fatal Duel, Says Don'. Or rather – (*sceptically*) 'Says Don!'

VALENTINE: It may all prove to be true.

HANNAH: It can't prove to be true, it can only not prove to be false yet.

VALENTINE: (*Pleased*) Just like science.

HANNAH: If Bernard can stay ahead of getting the rug pulled till he's dead, he'll be a success.

VALENTINE: *Just* like science . . . The ultimate fear is of posterity . . .

HANNAH: Personally I don't think it'll take that long.

VALENTINE: . . . and then there's the afterlife. An afterlife would be a mixed blessing. 'Ah – Bernard Nightingale, I don't believe you know Lord Byron.' It must be heaven up there.

HANNAH: You can't believe in an afterlife, Valentine.

VALENTINE: Oh, you're going to disappoint me at last.

HANNAH: Am I? Why?

VALENTINE: Science and religion.

HANNAH: No, no, been there, done that, boring.

VALENTINE: Oh, Hannah. Fiancée. Have pity. Can't we have a trial marriage and I'll call it off in the morning?

HANNAH: (*Amused*) I don't know when I've received a more unusual proposal.

VALENTINE: (*Interested*) Have you had many?

HANNAH: That would be telling.

VALENTINE: Well, why not? Your classical reserve is only a mannerism; and neurotic.

HANNAH: Do you want the room?

VALENTINE: You get nothing if you give nothing.

HANNAH: I ask nothing.

VALENTINE: No, stay.

(VALENTINE *resumes work at his computer.* HANNAH *establishes herself among her references at 'her' end of the table. She has a stack of pocket-sized volumes, Lady Croom's 'garden books'.*)

HANNAH: What are you doing? Valentine?

VALENTINE: The set of points on a complex plane made by –

HANNAH: Is it the grouse?

VALENTINE: Oh, the grouse. The damned grouse.

HANNAH: You mustn't give up.

VALENTINE: Why? Didn't you agree with Bernard?

HANNAH: Oh, that. It's *all* trivial – your grouse, my hermit, Bernard's Byron. Comparing what we're looking for misses the point. It's wanting to know that makes us matter. Otherwise we're going out the way we came in. That's why you can't believe in the afterlife, Valentine. Believe in the after, by all means, but not the life. Believe in God, the soul, the spirit, the infinite, believe in angels if you like, but not in the great celestial get-together for an exchange of views. If the answers are in the back of the book I can wait, but what a

drag. Better to struggle on knowing that failure is final.
(*She looks over* VALENTINE'*s shoulder at the computer screen.
Reacting*) Oh!, but . . . how beautiful!

VALENTINE: The Coverly set.

HANNAH: The Coverly set! My goodness, Valentine!

VALENTINE: Lend me a finger.
(*He takes her finger and presses one of the computer keys several
times.*)
See? In an ocean of ashes, islands of order. Patterns making
themselves out of nothing.
I can't show you how deep it goes. Each picture is a detail of the
previous one, blown up. And so on. For ever. Pretty nice, eh?

HANNAH: Is it important?

VALENTINE: Interesting. Publishable.

HANNAH: Well done!

VALENTINE: Not me. It's Thomasina's. I just pushed her
equations through the computer a few million times further
than she managed to do with her pencil.
(*From the old portfolio he takes Thomasina's lesson book and gives
it to* HANNAH. *The piano starts to be heard.*)
You can have it back now.

HANNAH: What does it mean?

VALENTINE: Not what you'd like it to.

HANNAH: Why not?

VALENTINE: Well, for one thing, she'd be famous.

HANNAH: No, she wouldn't. She was dead before she had time to
be famous . . .

VALENTINE: She died?

HANNAH: . . . burned to death.

VALENTINE: (*Realizing*) Oh . . . the girl who died in the fire!

HANNAH: The night before her seventeenth birthday. You can see
where the dormer doesn't match. That was her bedroom
under the roof. There's a memorial in the Park.

VALENTINE: (*Irritated*) I know – it's my house.
(VALENTINE *turns his attention back to his computer.* HANNAH
goes back to her chair. She looks through the lesson book.)

HANNAH: Val, Septimus was her tutor – he and Thomasina would
have –

VALENTINE: You do yours.
>   (*Pause. Two researchers.*

>   LORD AUGUSTUS, *fifteen years old, wearing clothes of 1812,
>   bursts in through the non-music room door. He is laughing. He
>   dives under the table. He is chased into the room by*
>   THOMASINA, *aged sixteen and furious. She spots* AUGUSTUS
>   *immediately.*)

THOMASINA: You swore! You crossed your heart!
>   (AUGUSTUS *scampers out from under the table and* THOMASINA
>   *chases him around it.*)

AUGUSTUS: I'll tell mama! I'll tell mama!

THOMASINA: You beast!
>   (*She catches* AUGUSTUS *as* SEPTIMUS *enters from the other
>   door, carrying a book, a decanter and a glass, and his portfolio.*)

SEPTIMUS: Hush! What is this? My lord! Order, order!
>   (THOMASINA *and* AUGUSTUS *separate.*)
>   I am obliged.
>   (SEPTIMUS *goes to his place at the table. He pours himself a
>   glass of wine.*)

AUGUSTUS: Well, good day to you, Mr Hodge!
>   (*He is smirking about something.*
>   THOMASINA *dutifully picks up a drawing book and settles down
>   to draw the geometrical solids.*
>   SEPTIMUS *opens his portfolio.*)

SEPTIMUS: Will you join us this morning, Lord Augustus? We
have our drawing lesson.

AUGUSTUS: I am a master of it at Eton, Mr Hodge, but we only
draw naked women.

SEPTIMUS: You may work from memory.

THOMASINA: Disgusting!

SEPTIMUS: We will have silence now, if you please.
>   (*From the portfolio* SEPTIMUS *takes Thomasina's lesson book
>   and tosses it to her; returning homework. She snatches it and
>   opens it.*)

THOMASINA: No marks?! Did you not like my rabbit equation?

SEPTIMUS: I saw no resemblance to a rabbit.

THOMASINA: It eats its own progeny.

SEPTIMUS: (*Pause*) I did not see that.

(*He extends his hand for the lesson book. She returns it to him.*)

THOMASINA: I have not room to extend it.

(SEPTIMUS *and* HANNAH *turn the pages doubled by time.*
AUGUSTUS *indolently starts to draw the models.*)

HANNAH: Do you mean the world is saved after all?

VALENTINE: No, it's still doomed. But if this is how it started, perhaps it's how the next one will come.

HANNAH: From good English algebra?

SEPTIMUS: It will go to infinity or zero, or nonsense.

THOMASINA: No, if you set apart the minus roots they square back to sense.

(SEPTIMUS *turns the pages.*
THOMASINA *starts drawing the models.*

HANNAH *closes the lesson book and turns her attention to her stack of 'garden books'.*)

VALENTINE: Listen – you know your tea's getting cold.

HANNAH: I like it cold.

VALENTINE: (*Ignoring that*) I'm telling you something. Your tea gets cold by itself, it doesn't get hot by itself. Do you think that's
odd?

HANNAH: No.

VALENTINE: Well, it is odd. Heat goes to cold. It's a one-way street. Your tea will end up at room temperature. What's happening to your tea is happening to everything everywhere. The sun and the stars. It'll take a while but we're all going to end up at room temperature. When your hermit set up shop nobody understood this. But let's say you're right, in 18-whatever nobody knew more about heat than this scribbling nutter living in a hovel in Derbyshire.

HANNAH: He was at Cambridge – a scientist.

VALENTINE: Say he was. I'm not arguing. And the girl was his pupil, she had a genius for her tutor.

HANNAH: Or the other way round.

VALENTINE: Anything you like. But not *this*! Whatever he thought he was doing to save the world with good English algebra it wasn't this!

HANNAH: Why? Because they didn't have calculators?

VALENTINE: No. Yes. Because there's an order things can't happen in. You can't open a door till there's a house.

HANNAH: I thought that's what genius was.

VALENTINE: Only for lunatics and poets.

(*Pause.*)

HANNAH: 'I had a dream which was not all a dream.

> The bright sun was extinguished, and the stars
> Did wander darkling in the eternal space,
> Rayless, and pathless, and the icy earth
> Swung blind and blackening in the moonless air . . .'

VALENTINE: Your own?

HANNAH: Byron.

(*Pause. Two researchers again.*)

THOMASINA: Septimus, do you think that I will marry Lord Byron?

AUGUSTUS: Who is he?

THOMASINA: He is the author of 'Childe Harold's Pilgrimage', the most poetical and pathetic and bravest hero of any book I ever read before, and the most modern and the handsomest, for Harold is Lord Byron himself to those who know him, like myself and Septimus. Well, Septimus?

SEPTIMUS: (*Absorbed*) No.

(*Then he puts her lesson book away into the portfolio and picks up his own book to read.*)

THOMASINA: Why not?

SEPTIMUS: For one thing, he is not aware of your existence.

THOMASINA: We exchanged many significant glances when he was at Sidley Park. I do wonder that he has been home almost a year from his adventures and has not written to me once.

SEPTIMUS: It is indeed improbable, my lady.

AUGUSTUS: Lord Byron?! – he claimed my hare, although my shot was the earlier! He said I missed by a hare's breadth. His conversation was very facetious. But I think Lord Byron will not marry you, Thom, for he was only lame and not blind.

SEPTIMUS: Peace! Peace until a quarter to twelve. It is intolerable for a tutor to have his thoughts interrupted by his pupils.

AUGUSTUS: You are not *my* tutor, sir. I am visiting your lesson by my free will.

SEPTIMUS: If you are so determined, my lord.

(THOMASINA *laughs at that, the joke is for her.* AUGUSTUS, *not included, becomes angry.*)

AUGUSTUS: Your peace is nothing to me, sir. You do not rule over me.

THOMASINA: (*Admonishing*) Augustus!

SEPTIMUS: I do not rule here, my lord. I inspire by reverence for learning and the exaltation of knowledge whereby man may approach God. There will be a shilling for the best cone and pyramid drawn in silence by a quarter to twelve *at the earliest.*

AUGUSTUS: You will not buy my silence for a shilling, sir. What I know to tell is worth much more than that.

(*And throwing down his drawing book and pencil, he leaves the room on his dignity, closing the door sharply. Pause.* SEPTIMUS *looks enquiringly at* THOMASINA.)

THOMASINA: I told him you kissed me. But he will not tell.

SEPTIMUS: When did I kiss you?

THOMASINA: What! Yesterday!

SEPTIMUS: Where?

THOMASINA: On the lips!

SEPTIMUS: In which county?

THOMASINA: In the hermitage, Septimus!

SEPTIMUS: On the lips in the hermitage! That? That was not a shilling kiss! I would not give sixpence to have it back. I had almost forgot it already.

THOMASINA: Oh, cruel! Have you forgotten our compact?

SEPTIMUS: God save me! Our compact?

THOMASINA: To teach me to waltz! Sealed with a kiss, and a second kiss due when I can dance like mama!

SEPTIMUS: Ah yes. Indeed. We were all waltzing like mice in London.

THOMASINA: I must waltz, Septimus! I will be despised if I do not waltz! It is the most fashionable and gayest and boldest invention conceivable – started in Germany!

SEPTIMUS: Let them have the waltz, they cannot have the calculus.

THOMASINA: Mama has brought from town a whole book of waltzes for the Broadwood, to play with Count Zelinsky.

SEPTIMUS: I need not be told what I cannot but suffer. Count Zelinsky banging on the Broadwood without relief has me reading in waltz time.

THOMASINA: Oh, stuff! What is your book?

SEPTIMUS: A prize essay of the Scientific Academy in Paris. The author deserves your indulgence, my lady, for you are his prophet.

THOMASINA: I? What does he write about? The waltz?

SEPTIMUS: Yes. He demonstrates the equation of the propagation of heat in a solid body. But in doing so he has discovered heresy – a natural contradiction of Sir Isaac Newton.

THOMASINA: Oh! – he contradicts determinism?

SEPTIMUS: No! . . . Well, perhaps. He shows that the atoms do not go according to Newton.

(Her interest has switched in the mercurial way characteristic of her – she has crossed to take the book.)

THOMASINA: Let me see – oh! In French?

SEPTIMUS: Yes. Paris is the capital of France.

THOMASINA: Show me where to read.

(He takes the book back from her and finds the page for her. Meanwhile, the piano music from the next room has doubled its notes and its emotion.)

THOMASINA: Four-handed now! Mama is in love with the Count.

SEPTIMUS: He is a Count in Poland. In Derbyshire he is a piano tuner.

(She has taken the book and is already immersed in it. The piano music becomes rapidly more passionate, and then breaks off suddenly in mid-phrase. There is an expressive silence next door which makes SEPTIMUS raise his eyes. It does not register with THOMASINA. The silence allows us to hear the distant regular thump of the steam engine which is to be a topic. A few moments later LADY CROOM enters from the music room, seeming surprised and slightly flustered to find the schoolroom occupied. She collects herself, closing the door behind her. And remains watching,

aimless and discreet, as though not wanting to interrupt the lesson.
SEPTIMUS *has stood, and she nods him back into his chair.*

CHLOË, *in Regency dress, enters from the door opposite the music
room. She takes in* VALENTINE *and* HANNAH *but crosses without
pausing to the music room door.*)
CHLOË: Oh! – where's Gus?
VALENTINE: Dunno.
    (CHLOË *goes into the music room.*)
LADY CROOM: (*Annoyed*) Oh! – Mr Noakes's engine!

    (*She goes to the garden door and steps outside.*
    CHLOË *re-enters.*)
CHLOË: Damn.
LADY CROOM: (*Calls out*) Mr Noakes!
VALENTINE: He was there not long ago . . .
LADY CROOM: Halloo!
CHLOË: Well, he has to be in the photograph – is he dressed?
HANNAH: Is Bernard back?
CHLOË: No – he's late!
    (*The piano is heard again, under the noise of the steam engine.*
    LADY CROOM *steps back into the room.*

    CHLOË *steps outside the garden door. Shouts.*) Gus!
LADY CROOM: I wonder you can teach against such a disturbance
    and I am sorry for it, Mr Hodge.
    (CHLOË *comes back inside.*)
VALENTINE: (*Getting up*) Stop ordering everybody about.
LADY CROOM: It is an unendurable noise.
VALENTINE: The photographer will wait.
    (*But, grumbling, he follows* CHLOË *out of the door she came in by,
    and closes the door behind them.* HANNAH *remains absorbed.
    In the silence, the rhythmic thump can be heard again.*)
LADY CROOM: The ceaseless dull overbearing monotony of it! It
    will drive me distracted. I may have to return to town to
    escape it.
SEPTIMUS: Your ladyship could remain in the country and let
    Count Zelinsky return to town where you would not hear him.
LADY CROOM: I mean Mr Noakes's engine! (*Semi-aside to*

82

SEPTIMUS.) Would you sulk? I will not have my daughter
study sulking.

THOMASINA: (*Not listening*) What, mama?

(THOMASINA *remains lost in her book.* LADY CROOM *returns to
close the garden door and the noise of the steam engine subsides.*

HANNAH *closes one of the 'garden books', and opens the next.
She is making occasional notes.*

The piano ceases.)

LADY CROOM: (*To* THOMASINA) What are we learning today?
(*Pause.*) Well, not manners.

SEPTIMUS: We are drawing today.

(LADY CROOM *negligently examines what* THOMASINA *had
started to draw.*)

LADY CROOM: Geometry. I approve of geometry.

SEPTIMUS: Your ladyship's approval is my constant object.

LADY CROOM: Well, do not despair of it. (*Returning to the window
impatiently.*) Where is 'Culpability' Noakes? (*She looks out
and is annoyed.*) Oh! – he has gone for his hat so that he may
remove it.

(*She returns to the table and touches the bowl of dahlias.*

HANNAH *sits back in her chair, caught by what she is reading.*)
For the widow's dowry of dahlias I can almost forgive my
brother's marriage. We must be thankful the monkey bit the
husband. If it had bit the wife the monkey would be dead
and we would not be first in the kingdom to show a dahlia.
(HANNAH, *still reading the garden book, stands up.*) I sent one
potted to Chatsworth. The Duchess was most satisfactorily
put out by it when I called at Devonshire House. Your friend
was there lording it as a poet.

(HANNAH *leaves through the door, following* VALENTINE *and*
CHLOË.)

Meanwhile, THOMASINA *thumps the book down on the table.*)

THOMASINA: Well! Just as I said! Newton's machine which
would knock our atoms from cradle to grave by the laws of
motion is incomplete! Determinism leaves the road at every
corner, as I knew all along, and the cause is very likely

hidden in this gentleman's observation.

LADY CROOM: Of what?

THOMASINA: The action of bodies in heat.

LADY CROOM: Is this geometry?

THOMASINA: This? No, I despise geometry!

LADY CROOM: (*Touching the dahlias she adds, almost to herself.*) The Chater would overthrow the Newtonian system in a weekend.

SEPTIMUS: Geometry, Hobbes assures us in the *Leviathan*, is the only science God has been pleased to bestow on mankind.

LADY CROOM: And what does he mean by it?

SEPTIMUS: Mr Hobbes or God?

LADY CROOM: I am sure I do not know what either means by it.

THOMASINA: Oh, pooh to Hobbes! Mountains are not pyramids and trees are not cones. God must love gunnery and architecture if Euclid is his only geometry. There is another geometry which I am engaged in discovering by trial and error, am I not, Septimus?

SEPTIMUS: Trial and error perfectly describes your enthusiasm, my lady.

LADY CROOM: How old are you today?

THOMASINA: Sixteen years and eleven months, mama, and three weeks.

LADY CROOM: Sixteen years and eleven months. We must have you married before you are educated beyond eligibility.

THOMASINA: I am going to marry Lord Byron.

LADY CROOM: Are you? He did not have the manners to mention it.

THOMASINA: You have spoken to him?!

LADY CROOM: Certainly not.

THOMASINA: Where did you see him?

LADY CROOM: (*With some bitterness*) Everywhere.

THOMASINA: Did you, Septimus?

SEPTIMUS: At the Royal Academy where I had the honour to accompany your mother and Count Zelinsky.

THOMASINA: What was Lord Byron doing?

LADY CROOM: Posing.

SEPTIMUS: (*Tactfully*) He was being sketched during his visit . . .

by the Professor of Painting . . . Mr Fuseli.

LADY CROOM: There was more posing *at* the pictures than *in* them. His companion likewise reversed the custom of the Academy that the ladies viewing wear more than the ladies viewed – well, enough! Let him be hanged there for a Lamb. I have enough with Mr Noakes, who is to a garden what a bull is to a china shop.

(*This as* NOAKES *enters.*)

THOMASINA: The Emperor of Irregularity!

(*She settles down to drawing the diagram which is to be the third item in the surviving portfolio.*)

LADY CROOM: Mr Noakes!

NOAKES: Your ladyship –

LADY CROOM: What have you done to me!

NOAKES: Everything is satisfactory, I assure you. A little behind, to be sure, but my dam will be repaired within the month –

LADY CROOM: (*Banging the table*) Hush!

(*In the silence, the steam engine thumps in the distance.*)

Can you hear, Mr Noakes?

NOAKES: (*Pleased and proud*) The Improved Newcomen steam pump – the only one in England!

LADY CROOM: That is what I object to. If everybody had his own I would bear my portion of the agony without complaint. But to have been singled out by the only Improved Newcomen steam pump in England, this is hard, sir, this is not to be borne.

NOAKES: Your lady –

LADY CROOM: And for what? My lake is drained to a ditch for no purpose I can understand, unless it be that snipe and curlew have deserted three counties so that they may be shot in our swamp. What you painted as forest is a mean plantation, your greenery is mud, your waterfall is wet mud, and your mount is an opencast mine for the mud that was lacking in the dell. (*Pointing through the window.*) What is that cowshed?

NOAKES: The hermitage, my lady?

LADY CROOM: It is a cowshed.

NOAKES: Madam, it is, I assure you, a very habitable cottage, properly founded and drained, two rooms and a closet under a slate roof and a stone chimney –

LADY CROOM: And who is to live in it?

NOAKES: Why, the hermit.

LADY CROOM: Where is he?

NOAKES: Madam?

LADY CROOM: You surely do not supply a hermitage without a hermit?

NOAKES: Indeed, madam –

LADY CROOM: Come, come, Mr Noakes. If I am promised a fountain I expect it to come with water. What hermits do you have?

NOAKES: I have no hermits, my lady.

LADY CROOM: Not one? I am speechless.

NOAKES: I am sure a hermit can be found. One could advertise.

LADY CROOM: Advertise?

NOAKES: In the newspapers.

LADY CROOM: But surely a hermit who takes a newspaper is not a hermit in whom one can have complete confidence.

NOAKES: I do not know what to suggest, my lady.

SEPTIMUS: Is there room for a piano?

NOAKES: (*Baffled*) A piano?

LADY CROOM: We are intruding here – this will not do, Mr Hodge. Evidently, nothing is being learned. (*To* NOAKES) Come along, sir!

THOMASINA: Mr Noakes – bad news from Paris!

NOAKES: Is it the Emperor Napoleon?

THOMASINA: No. (*She tears the page off her drawing block, with her 'diagram' on it.*) It concerns your heat engine. Improve it as you will, you can never get out of it what you put in. It repays eleven pence in the shilling at most. The penny is for this author's thoughts.

(*She gives the diagram to* SEPTIMUS *who looks at it.*)

NOAKES: (*Baffled again*) Thank you, my lady.

(NOAKES *goes out into the garden.*)

LADY CROOM: (To SEPTIMUS) Do you understand her?

SEPTIMUS: No.

LADY CROOM: Then this business is over. I was married at

seventeen. *Ce soir il faut qu'on parle français, je te demande,* Thomasina, as a courtesy to the Count. Wear your green velvet, please, I will send Briggs to do your hair. Sixteen and eleven months . . .!

(*She follows* NOAKES *out of view.*)

THOMASINA: Lord Byron was with a lady?

SEPTIMUS: Yes.

THOMASINA: Huh!

(*Now* SEPTIMUS *retrieves his book from* THOMASINA. *He turns the pages, and also continues to study Thomasina's diagram. He strokes the tortoise absently as he reads.* THOMASINA *takes up pencil and paper and starts to draw* SEPTIMUS *with Plautus.*)

SEPTIMUS: Why does it mean Mr Noakes's engine pays eleven pence in the shilling? Where does he say it?

THOMASINA: Nowhere. I noticed it by the way. I cannot remember now.

SEPTIMUS: Nor is he interested by determinism –

THOMASINA: Oh . . . yes. Newton's equations go forwards and backwards, they do not care which way. But the heat equation cares very much, it goes only one way. That is the reason Mr Noakes's engine cannot give the power to drive Mr Noakes's engine.

SEPTIMUS: Everybody knows that.

THOMASINA: Yes, Septimus, they know it about engines!

SEPTIMUS: (*Pause. He looks at his watch.*) A quarter to twelve. For your essay this week, explicate your diagram.

THOMASINA: I cannot. I do not know the mathematics.

SEPTIMUS: Without mathematics, then.

(THOMASINA *has continued to draw. She tears the top page from her drawing pad and gives it to* SEPTIMUS.)

THOMASINA: There. I have made a drawing of you and Plautus.

SEPTIMUS: (*Looking at it*) Excellent likeness. Not so good of me.

(THOMASINA *laughs, and leaves the room.*

AUGUSTUS *appears at the garden door. His manner cautious and diffident.* SEPTIMUS *does not notice him for a moment.*

SEPTIMUS *gathers his papers together.*)

AUGUSTUS: Sir . . .

SEPTIMUS: My lord . . .?

87

AUGUSTUS: I gave you offence, sir, and I am sorry for it.

SEPTIMUS: I took none, my lord, but you are kind to mention it.

AUGUSTUS: I would like to ask you a question, Mr Hodge. (*Pause.*) You have an elder brother, I dare say, being a Septimus?

SEPTIMUS: Yes, my lord. He lives in London. He is the editor of a newspaper, the *Piccadilly Recreation*. (*Pause.*) Was that your question?

(AUGUSTUS, *evidently embarrassed about something, picks up the drawing of Septimus.*)

AUGUSTUS: No. Oh . . . it is you? . . . I would like to keep it. (SEPTIMUS *inclines his head in assent.*) There are things a fellow cannot ask his friends. Carnal things. My sister has told me . . . my sister believes such things as I cannot, I assure you, bring myself to repeat.

SEPTIMUS: You must not repeat them, then. The walk between here and dinner will suffice to put us straight, if we stroll by the garden. It is an easy business. And then I must rely on you to correct your sister's state of ignorance.

(*A commotion is heard outside* – BERNARD's *loud voice in a sort of agony.*)

BERNARD: (*outside the door*) Oh no – no – no – oh, bloody hell! –

AUGUSTUS: Thank you, Mr Hodge, I will.

(*Taking the drawing with him,* AUGUSTUS *allows himself to be shown out through the garden door, and* SEPTIMUS *follows him.*

BERNARD *enters the room, through the door* HANNAH *left by.* VALENTINE *comes in with him, leaving the door open and they are followed by* HANNAH *who is holding the 'garden book'.*)

BERNARD: Oh, no – no –

HANNAH: I'm sorry, Bernard.

BERNARD: Fucked by a dahlia! Do you think? Is it open and shut? Am I fucked? What does it really amount to? When all's said and done? Am I fucked? What do *you* think, Valentine? Tell me the truth.

VALENTINE: You're fucked.

BERNARD: Oh God! Does it mean that?

HANNAH: Yes, Bernard, it does.

BERNARD: I'm not sure. Show me where it says. I want to see it. No – read it – no, wait . . .

(BERNARD *sits at the table. He prepares to listen as though listening were an oriental art.*)

Right.

HANNAH: (*Reading*) 'October 1st, 1810. Today under the direction of Mr Noakes, a parterre was dug on the south lawn and will be a handsome show next year, a consolation for the picturesque catastrophe of the second and third distances. The dahlia having propagated under glass with no ill effect from the sea voyage, is named by Captain Brice 'Charity' for his bride, though the honour properly belongs to the husband who exchanged beds with my dahlia, and an English summer for everlasting night in the Indies.'

(*Pause.*)

BERNARD: Well it's so round the houses, isn't it? Who's to say what it means?

HANNAH: (*Patiently*) It means that Ezra Chater of the Sidley Park connection is the same Chater who described a dwarf dahlia in Martinique in 1810 and died there, of a monkey bite.

BERNARD: (*Wildly*) Ezra wasn't a botanist! He was a poet!

HANNAH: He was not much of either, but he was both.

VALENTINE: It's not a disaster.

BERNARD: Of course it's a disaster! I was on 'The Breakfast Hour'!

VALENTINE: It doesn't mean Byron didn't fight a duel, it only means Chater wasn't killed in it.

BERNARD: Oh, pull yourself together! – do you think I'd have been on 'The Breakfast Hour' if Byron had *missed*!

HANNAH: Calm down, Bernard. Valentine's right.

BERNARD: (*Grasping at straws*) Do you think so? You mean the *Piccadilly* reviews? Yes, two completely unknown Byron essays – *and* my discovery of the lines he added to 'English Bards'. That counts for something.

HANNAH: (*Tactfully*) Very possible – persuasive, indeed.

BERNARD: Oh, bugger persuasive! I've proved Byron was here and as far as I'm concerned he wrote those lines as sure as he shot that hare. If only I hadn't somehow . . . made it all about *killing Chater*. Why didn't you stop me?! It's bound to get out, you know – I mean this – this *gloss* on my discovery – I mean how long do you think it'll be before some botanical pedant blows the whistle on me?

HANNAH: The day after tomorrow. A letter in *The Times*.

BERNARD: You wouldn't.

HANNAH: It's a dirty job but somebody –

BERNARD: Darling. Sorry. Hannah –

HANNAH: – and, after all, it is my discovery.

BERNARD: Hannah.

HANNAH: Bernard.

BERNARD: Hannah.

HANNAH: Oh, shut up. It'll be very short, very dry, absolutely gloat-free. Would you rather it were one of your friends?

BERNARD: (*Fervently*) Oh God, no!

HANNAH: And then in *your* letter to *The Times* –

BERNARD: Mine?

HANNAH: Well, of course. Dignified congratulations to a colleague, in the language of scholars, I trust.

BERNARD: Oh, eat shit, you mean?

HANNAH: Think of it as a breakthrough in dahlia studies.
(CHLOË *hurries in from the garden.*)

CHLOË: Why aren't you coming?! – Bernard! And you're not dressed! How long have you been back?
(BERNARD *looks at her and then at* VALENTINE *and realizes for the first time that* VALENTINE *is unusually dressed.*)

BERNARD: Why are you wearing those clothes?

CHLOË: Do be quick!
(*She is already digging into the basket and producing odd garments for* BERNARD.)
Just put anything on. We're all being photographed. Except Hannah.

HANNAH: I'll come and watch.
(VALENTINE *and* CHLOË *help* BERNARD *into a decorative coat and fix a lace collar round his neck.*)

CHLOË: (*To* HANNAH) Mummy says have you got the theodolite?

VALENTINE: What are you supposed to be, Chlo? Bo-Peep?

CHLOË: Jane Austen!

VALENTINE: Of course.

HANNAH: (*To* CHLOË) Oh – it's in the hermitage! Sorry.

BERNARD: I thought it wasn't till this evening. What photograph?

CHLOË: The local paper of course – they always come before we start. We want a good crowd of us – Gus looks gorgeous –

BERNARD: (*Aghast*) The newspaper!

(*He grabs something like a bishop's mitre from the basket and pulls it down completely over his face.*

(*Muffled*) I'm ready!

(*And he staggers out with* VALENTINE *and* CHLOË, *followed by* HANNAH.

A light change to evening. The paper lanterns outside begin to glow. Piano music from the next room.

SEPTIMUS *enters with an oil lamp. He carries Thomasina's algebra primer, and also her essay on loose sheets. He settles down to read at the table. It is nearly dark outside, despite the lanterns.*

THOMASINA *enters, in a nightgown and barefoot, holding a candlestick. Her manner is secretive and excited.*)

SEPTIMUS: My lady! What is it?

THOMASINA: Septimus! Shush!

(*She closes the door quietly.*)

Now is our chance!

SEPTIMUS: For what, dear God?

(*She blows out the candle and puts the candlestick on the table.*)

THOMASINA: Do not act the innocent! Tomorrow I will be seventeen!

(*She kisses* SEPTIMUS *full on the mouth.*)

There!

SEPTIMUS: Dear Christ!

THOMASINA: Now you must show me, you are paid in advance.

SEPTIMUS: (*Understanding*) Oh!

THOMASINA: The Count plays for us, it is God-given! I cannot be seventeen and not waltz.

SEPTIMUS: But your mother –

THOMASINA: While she swoons, we can dance. The house is all abed. I heard the Broadwood. Oh, Septimus, teach me now!

SEPTIMUS: Hush! I cannot now!

THOMASINA: Indeed you can, and I am come barefoot so mind my toes.

SEPTIMUS: I cannot because it is not a waltz.

THOMASINA: It is not?

SEPTIMUS: No, it is too slow for waltzing.

THOMASINA: Oh! Then we will wait for him to play quickly.

SEPTIMUS: My lady –

THOMASINA: Mr Hodge!

(*She takes a chair next to him and looks at his work.*)

Are you reading my essay? Why do you work here so late?

SEPTIMUS: To save my candles.

THOMASINA: You have my old primer.

SEPTIMUS: It is mine again. You should not have written in it.

(*She takes it, looks at the open page.*)

THOMASINA: It was a joke.

SEPTIMUS: It will make me mad as you promised. Sit over there. You will have us in disgrace.

(THOMASINA *gets up and goes to the furthest chair.*)

THOMASINA: If mama comes I will tell her we only met to kiss, not to waltz.

SEPTIMUS: Silence or bed.

THOMASINA: Silence!

(SEPTIMUS *pours himself some more wine. He continues to read her essay.*

The music changes to party music from the marquee. And there are fireworks – small against the sky, distant flares of light like exploding meteors.

HANNAH *enters. She has dressed for the party. The difference is not, however, dramatic. She closes the door and crosses to leave by the garden door. But as she gets there,* VALENTINE *is entering. He has a glass of wine in his hand.*)

HANNAH: Oh . . .

(*But* VALENTINE *merely brushes past her, intent on something, and half-drunk.*)

VALENTINE: (*To her*) Got it!

(*He goes straight to the table and roots about in what is now a considerable mess of papers, books and objects.* HANNAH *turns back, puzzled by his manner. He finds what he has been looking for – the 'diagram'.*

Meanwhile, SEPTIMUS *reading Thomasina's essay, also studies the diagram.*

SEPTIMUS *and* VALENTINE *study the diagram doubled by time.*)

VALENTINE: It's heat.

HANNAH: Are you tight, Val?

VALENTINE: It's a diagram of heat exchange.

SEPTIMUS: So, we are all doomed!

THOMASINA: (*Cheerfully*) Yes.

VALENTINE: Like a steam engine, you see –

(HANNAH *fills Septimus's glass from the same decanter, and sips from it.*)

She didn't have the maths, not remotely. She saw what things meant, way ahead, like seeing a picture.

SEPTIMUS: This is not science. This is story-telling.

THOMASINA: Is it a waltz now?

SEPTIMUS: No.

(*The music is still modern.*)

VALENTINE: Like a film.

HANNAH: What did she see?

VALENTINE: That you can't run the film backwards. Heat was the first thing which didn't work that way. Not like Newton. A film of a pendulum, or a ball falling through the air – backwards, it looks the same.

HANNAH: The ball would be going the wrong way.

VALENTINE: You'd have to know that. But with heat – friction – a ball breaking a window –

HANNAH: Yes.

VALENTINE: It won't work backwards.

HANNAH: Who thought it did?

VALENTINE: She saw why. You can put back the bits of glass but you can't collect up the heat of the smash. It's gone.

SEPTIMUS: So the Improved Newtonian Universe must cease and grow cold. Dear me.

VALENTINE: The heat goes into the mix.

(*He gestures to indicate the air in the room, in the universe.*)

THOMASINA: Yes, we must hurry if we are going to dance.

VALENTINE: And everything is mixing the same way, all the time, irreversibly . . .

SEPTIMUS: Oh, we have time, I think.

VALENTINE: . . . till there's no time left. That's what time means.

SEPTIMUS: When we have found all the mysteries and lost all the meaning, we will be alone, on an empty shore.

THOMASINA: Then we will dance. Is this a waltz?

SEPTIMUS: It will serve.

(*He stands up.*)

THOMASINA: (*Jumping up*) Goody!

(SEPTIMUS *takes her in his arms carefully and the waltz lesson, to the music from the marquee, begins.*

BERNARD, *in unconvincing Regency dress, enters carrying a bottle.*)

BERNARD: Don't mind me, I left my jacket . . .

(*He heads for the area of the wicker basket.*)

VALENTINE: Are you leaving?

(BERNARD *is stripping off his period coat. He is wearing his own trousers, tucked into knee socks and his own shirt.*)

BERNARD: Yes, I'm afraid so.

HANNAH: What's up, Bernard?

BERNARD: Nothing I can go into –

VALENTINE: Should I go?

BERNARD: No, *I'm* going!

(VALENTINE *and* HANNAH *watch* BERNARD *struggling into his jacket and adjusting his clothes.*

SEPTIMUS, *holding* THOMASINA, *kisses her on the mouth. The waltz lesson pauses. She looks at him. He kisses her again, in earnest. She puts her arms round him.*)

THOMASINA: Septimus . . .

(SEPTIMUS *hushes her. They start to dance again, with the slight awkwardness of a lesson.*

CHLOË *bursts in from the garden.*)

CHLOË: I'll kill her! I'll *kill* her!

BERNARD: Oh dear.

VALENTINE: What the hell is it, Chlo?

CHLOË: (*Venomously*) Mummy!

BERNARD: (*To* VALENTINE) Your mother caught us in that cottage.

CHLOË: She snooped!

BERNARD: I don't think so. She was rescuing a theodolite.

CHLOË: I'll come with you, Bernard.

BERNARD: No, you bloody won't.

CHLOË: Don't you want me to?

BERNARD: Of course not. What for? (*To* VALENTINE) I'm sorry.

CHLOË: (*In furious tears*) What are you saying sorry to *him* for?

BERNARD: Sorry to you too. Sorry one and all. Sorry, Hannah – sorry, Hermione – sorry, Byron – sorry, sorry, sorry, now can I go?

(CHLOË *stands stiffly, tearfully.*)

CHLOË: Well . . .

(THOMASINA *and* SEPTIMUS *dance.*)

HANNAH: What a bastard you are, Bernard.

(CHLOË *rounds on her.*)

CHLOË: And you mind your own business! What do you know about anything?

HANNAH: Nothing.

CHLOË: (*to* BERNARD) It *was* worth it, though, wasn't it?

BERNARD: It was wonderful.

(CHLOË *goes out, through the garden door, towards the party.*)

HANNAH: (*An echo*) Nothing.

VALENTINE: Well, you shit. I'd drive you but I'm a bit sloshed.

(VALENTINE *follows* CHLOË *out and can be heard outside calling 'Chlo! Chlo!'*)

BERNARD: A scrape.

HANNAH: Oh . . . (*she gives up*) Bernard!

BERNARD: I look forward to *The Genius of the Place*. I hope you find your hermit. I think out front is the safest.

(*He opens the door cautiously and looks out.*)

HANNAH: Actually, I've got a good idea who he was, but I can't prove it.

95

BERNARD: (*With a carefree expansive gesture*) Publish!
(*He goes out closing the door.*

SEPTIMUS *and* THOMASINA *are now waltzing freely. She is
delighted with herself.*)
THOMASINA: Am I waltzing?
SEPTIMUS: Yes, my lady.
(*He gives her a final twirl, bringing them to the table where he
bows to her. He lights her candlestick.*

HANNAH *goes to sit at the table, playing truant from the party.
She pours herself more wine. The table contains the geometrical
solids, the computer, decanter, glasses, tea mug, Hannah's
research books, Septimus's books, the two portfolios,
Thomasina's candlestick, the oil lamp, the dahlia, the Sunday
papers . . .*
GUS *appears in the doorway. It takes a moment to realize that he
is not Lord Augustus; perhaps not until* HANNAH *sees him.*)
SEPTIMUS: Take your essay, I have given it an alpha in blind
faith. Be careful with the flame.
THOMASINA: I will wait for you to come.
SEPTIMUS: I cannot.
THOMASINA: You may.
SEPTIMUS: I may not.
THOMASINA: You must.
SEPTIMUS: I will not.
(*She puts the candlestick and the essay on the table.*)
THOMASINA: Then I will not go. Once more, for my birthday.
(SEPTIMUS *and* THOMASINA *start to waltz together.*

GUS *comes forward, startling* HANNAH.)
HANNAH: Oh! – you made me jump.
(GUS *looks resplendent. He is carrying an old and somewhat
tattered stiff-backed folio fastened with a tape tied in a bow. He
comes to* HANNAH *and thrusts this present at her.*)
Oh . .
(*She lays the folio down on the table and starts to open it. It
consists only of two boards hinged, containing Thomasina's
drawing.*)

'Septimus holding Plautus'. (*To* GUS) I was looking for that. Thank you.

(GUS *nods several times. Then, rather awkwardly, he bows to her. A Regency bow, an invitation to dance.*)

Oh, dear, I don't really . . .

(*After a moment's hesitation, she gets up and they hold each other, keeping a decorous distance between them, and start to dance, rather awkwardly.*

SEPTIMUS *and* THOMASINA *continue to dance, fluently, to the piano.*)

END